OFF THE PEW, INTO THE WORLD

STARVING JESUS

CRAIG GROSS | J.R. MAHON

David C Cook®

transforming lives together

STARVING JESUS

Published by David C. Cook
4050 Lee Vance View
Colorado Springs, CO 80918 U.S.A.

David C. Cook Distribution Canada
55 Woodslee Avenue, Paris, Ontario, Canada N3L 3E5

David C. Cook U.K., Kingsway Communications
Eastbourne, East Sussex BN23 6NT, England

David C. Cook and the graphic circle C logo
are registered trademarks of Cook Communications Ministries.

The Web site addresses recommended throughout this book are offered as a
resource to you. These Web sites are not intended in any way to be or imply an
endorsement on the part of David C. Cook, nor do we vouch for their content.

All Scripture quotations, unless otherwise noted, are taken from the *Holy Bible,
New International Version*®. *NIV*®. Copyright © 1973, 1984 by International Bible
Society. Used by permission of Zondervan. All rights reserved. Scripture quota-
tions marked KJV are from the King James Version of the Bible. (Public Domain.)

LCCN 2007934656
ISBN 978-0-7814-4548-1
© 2007 Craig Gross and J.R. Mahon
Fireproof Ministries/XXXchurch.com
www.starvingjesus.com
P.O. Box 150169
Grand Rapids, MI 49515
Previously published under the same title © Gross & Mahon, ISBN 0-9741849-1-8.

The Team: Andrea Christian, John Blase, Theresa With, and Susan Vannaman
Cover Design: The DesignWorks Group
Cover Photo: Steve Gardner, PixelWorks Studios

Printed in the United States of America
Second Edition, 2007

1 2 3 4 5 6 7 8 9 10

080607

CONTENTS

ACKNOWLEDGMENTS

Thanks to our wives, Jeanette and Diane, for always listening and putting up with us. Thanks to Rob Supan for listening to the rant. Thanks to Mike DeVries for believing in this project. Thanks to Adam Palmer for editing this madness. And thanks to Mission Year and Compassion for doing what you do.

The following is a conversation between
Craig Gross & **J.R. Mahon**

INTRO | STARVING JESUS DEFINED

We were in Dallas one weekend giving a porn talk. Afterward, a few of the pastors and their wives who had listened to our talk invited J.R. and me to lunch. Never turn down a free lunch.

CHRISTIANS' INABILITY TO GET THINGS DONE

I was sitting across from one of the pastors' wives. She was a great lady with a wonderful personality, but she just didn't get it. J.R. explained to those at the table how we had helped a porn star get out of that business and raised $14,000 to help get her life together. It was a rewarding and wonderful example of how God works when people step forward to help others. To know God had used us to help this woman find redemption and start a new life in Christ was a great and humbling testimony for us to share.

This nice, southern, evangelical Christian pastor's wife looked across the table with her beautiful smile and well-intentioned life and stopped the gospel dead: "No matter what you or others do, God would have taken care of it if he wanted it done. It doesn't matter if you gave her money or not, God would have taken care of it if he wanted."

My jaw hit the table as she finished her sentence and smiled at us as if she had just dispensed the greatest Christian wisdom since Christ hung on the cross. I grabbed for my coffee cup and silently prayed, *Lord, don't let me kill this lady.*

"So basically, it's okay to look the other way when we see others in need?" I asked politely.

"If God wants something done, he will do it," she said with a smug righteousness.

J.R. buried his fork in his napkin, which was translation for, *Lord, don't let me kill this lady.* We think a lot alike.

I leaned forward. "If we all adopted that way of thinking, then the Bible becomes a moot point." She smiled. I just about vomited all over the table. Moments like that suck.

CHAPTER 1
TEND, NOT TALK

CH 1 | TEND, NOT TALK

Some conversations have a way of finding an audience. Some excite, some anger, some become the rule for the cause. Some are a colossal waste of time. Others, we pray, continue into eternity.

1.1
THE TALK

This particular conversation is going on right now. It starts and stops with every possible argument, thought, and dissertation we have for why church is the way it is. As believers, we hold this conversation close as we gather safely in our places of worship across this great country.

This conversation is usually kept behind closed doors. It's held between men and women who rarely deal with the unsaved and unchurched, people who have forgotten what the outside world looks like, smells like, and feels like.

This conversation has no affiliation to any one body of organized religion or faith. It's not evangelical, postmodern, emergent, left wing, or right wing. It has no PowerPoint presentation, and it has no line of ancillary products or T-shirts.

When this conversation begins, it questions, then reveals the painful truth about who Christians are as a church.

They start like this:

"Where is the love?"

"Why are we stuck in the pews?"

"Why is Sunday the only time we see Christians?"

"Why is everyone such a hypocrite?"

On rare occasions there are those willing to commit a form of spiritual suicide in the Christian subculture. Men and women yell from the rooftops, "Church sucks!" Their voices are quickly dismissed and rarely see the light of day. They are labeled fanatics and troublemakers and are asked not to come back.

Christ yelled the same type of thing once. It got him killed.

This conversation is on the tips of all sorts of tongues:

your fellow churchgoers, your neighbors, your spouse, your kids, your friends. And the most important part of this conversation is what *you* will say.

Welcome to the conversation.

JAMES 1:21 *Therefore, get rid of all moral filth and the evil that is so prevalent and humbly accept the word planted in you, which can save you.*

1.2
HONESTLY
CRAIG

I didn't go to church for years. I am an ordained minister—I grew up in the church—but ever since I left my job as a youth pastor, it was tough to go back.

"I love football." "I like to sleep in." "I would like a weekend off." "I can't sit through that boring service." I used all the excuses. "I don't need more corporate worship in my life." "I spend most of my weekends at church gatherings, conferences, and church events. When I'm home for a weekend, it's kind of nice to sit back and relax." For the first four years of my walk in full-time ministry, it was tough to attend church.

Rarely would I tell people that I did not go to church, but the few times I did, I almost always got the same reaction: concern. People were concerned for my family and me. They chimed in with their opinion on the subject (not because I asked for it; they just gave it). It didn't matter that I know every rendition of "Lord, I Lift Your Name on High" and have heard and given more messages from the pulpit in four years than many people will hear in a lifetime.

"You don't go to *church*?" they'd say, shocked. And the people asking me this question were the ones who would never allow me close enough to them. But they go to church.

Why didn't I go to church? The reason was simple: I didn't want to.

But one day I decided I would go. Because church is not about me, right? It is not about what *I* like, what *I* want to sing, what *I* wish I could hear, and how short *I* wish the service was. Sure, I have grown some. I have a family now and a wife who spends more time at home on the weekends than I do and who wants to connect with people other than just her husband.

Bottom line: I decided to go back to church to be a part of the solution. To borrow an analogy from sports: You can't get anything done when you're not on the field. The bench, the sideline, and the on-deck circle are a lot different than the court, the field, and the plate.

I have been a part of two new church communities in the last three years. I don't agree with everything they have done, but I don't have to. As I said, church is not about me; it is about all of us.

1.3
HONESTLY J.R.

I'll admit it: I have a hard time with most Christians. Most make me sick. The toothy grins, the mixed bag of fake and highly suspect promises. I love the church but hate its politics. I love the gathering but hate the process. I love the principles but hate the personalities.

Sinful thinking? Absolutely. I acknowledge it, and more times than not, I'm asking forgiveness for it. I pray God helps me through this crap; I pray for love in my life; I pray my heart softens to *all* of his children. I pray that I will see *you* the way Christ saw *me* when he went to the cross.

I first saw Christ when I was a teenager. I will spare you the details, but here's the nutshell version: I fell flat when I was eighteen, drug addicted, alcohol soaked, and morbidly morbid. Christ knocked, and with the little energy I had, I opened the door. It was hard, painful, joyful, crappy, funny, exhausting ... peaceful. I was changed forever through very little effort. All I did was lay my life down for a God I still have never seen, never touched, and never met in person. Crazy, right?

For those of you who think Christ was the inevitable last stop for a guy prone to addiction, you're right. I know the argument. I also know a few of you actually believe that only the shallow, weak-willed people of the world fall in love with Christ. That's true too.

I am quite content these days. In fact, I'm unbelievably peaceful. I no longer search for the next great thing to make me happy or get me going. I no longer yearn for things to make me satisfied. I am completely at peace with God.

Please note again: I'm at peace with God. That's important to know, because while I'm at peace with him, I am not completely peaceful with all the human beings around me, and some of them I don't even know. The bottom line is that God the Father has filled me with his Spirit, and I'm adjusting as I go.

I am a sinner and a Christian. Sometimes those words are reversed in my day-to-day existence, but for the most part that's what I am. I am on a quest to understand my human condition in relation to my spiritual condition. Basically I'm just like you, if you also care about a guy who hung bloody on a cross.

1.4
WHO ARE
THESE GUYS?

Here are a couple of questions: How can a porn pastor and a self-proclaimed street theologian have an opinion about the organized church? How can God take two sharp, edgy, politically incorrect voices that have a penchant for all things offensive and do anything with them?

We ask ourselves the same questions. We wonder why we talk about the things we do, why we resent the things we do, why we have to be involved in some of the most insane things going on in this crazy little subculture.

Here are two more good questions: Why do things stay so veiled and hidden in church circles? (We wonder why the church doesn't talk about sex, drugs, booze, lying, stealing, cheating.) Why do we insist on running away from sin?

We're like many of you. We still doubt God at times. We fight coveting the cool stuff other people have. We occasionally think we're not good enough. We wonder why God answers some prayers and not others. We get scared when we witness to people. We sometimes slack on our study and prayers. We even dream about taking a spiritual vacation: the kind that doesn't involve praying, studying, helping, dying to self, and digging sin out of our lives. It does sound good.

But sin—why can't we take sin head-on in the church? Why do we whisper about sin, creating layer after layer of shame for those struggling with it? Why are sinners running to self-help groups, reading books by doctors who have never seen a Bible, and logging hours with counselors who charge by the obsession?

Our leaders are doing everything they can to guide us into the good life by placating our sinful natures. We need some good old-fashioned butt kicking in the form of honest talk—and not just in the Wednesday night small group. We need it on Sunday mornings in the open, so the people—and there are many of us—enslaved to sin can get up and say, "Thank God someone finally said something!"

1.5

THE FATE OF

THE WORLD

For more than a year, J.R. and I have traveled all over the country. We have seen both the very best and the very dreadful in church activities. When not traveling, we tend to be on the phone with one another, determining the fate of the world through an ongoing conversation about faith and the church. We're pretty much resigned to the fact that the church is killing itself.

This may sound pessimistic, but it just doesn't seem as if we're getting anything done. We don't see a lot of love or compassion, and rarely do we read about the church reaching into the human gutter of sin and pulling people out. Just a lot of sanctimonious speech and self-righteous indignation, all wrapped up in great marketing and advertising. There's a whole lot of talk but not a whole lot of action.

Too harsh? Maybe. But the seeming lack of everything really bums us out. Yet in some sick way it puts smiles on our faces. We take some kind of weird pleasure in knowing the church is tanking, at least in its current form.

We're sick of the mega-Bible studies with postmodern

verbiage, coupled with poetry and art parties for the "emergent." We wonder what happened to evangelism. What happened to talking about the Bible as God's Word? Or prayers that end in "amen," instead of some long dissertation about being a speck of dust to his infinite hugeness.

We're sick of something we call Value Meal Theology. You may not know this, but pastors all over the country are choosing their sermons and lessons from the spiritual-message buffets cooked up by a few of the leading megachurches.

Pastors are closing the door on the creative force of the Holy Spirit within their own community in favor of Value Meal Theology. Why create something new when you can use another pastor's words, along with his well-established marketing teams, great hair products, and cool, untucked shirts? If *he* looks good and sounds good, then I can imitate him and *I'll* be good. Why let the inspiration of the Holy Spirit drive the message to the people in your own church when you can get a yearlong subscription to a great, feel-good, give-and-get program wrapped up with a bow, guaranteeing bigger and better results for your church? Never mind challenging yourself in the Word of God when you can shut yourself down on all fronts with another guy's message. After all, if you're having trouble increasing the numbers, go for what works.

We're sick of pastors with planes, pastors with record deals, pastors with bodyguards, pastors who offer time alone with them (for a fee), pastors with head shots.

What happened to pastors with sexual-sin problems? Bring back Jimmy Swaggart and Jim Bakker. At least we knew what we were getting. We're sick of not seeing Jesus in the pulpit. Instead, many of us are getting a weasely, feel-good message veiled with Scripture, so people won't run from the ten-million-dollar building.

We're sick of it! And yet ... happy. We're happy because something is on the horizon, and it's not offering the five keys to spiritual freedom. It's a mad army of disciples who are just like us: sick and tired of the shepherds who only *talk* to their flock and don't *tend* it. Alcoholics Anonymous refers to the apathy as being "sick and tired of being sick and tired."

We know a lot of this rhetoric will fall on deaf ears. For some of you, this doesn't apply—you have or are an awesome pastor who truly desires to hear God and follow him. For others, you're hunkered down in your beliefs and aren't going to hear us, no matter what we say.

We know we can't write the definitive book on how to change church culture, because we hear the arguments all the time. One person says the church needs a bomb to shake it up. Others say, "Change? We don't need to change, we're doing great!"

Look, there are facts, figures, and statistics we could roll out at this point, but we're not Barna. We'll take our chances with the Holy Spirit. We're stepping out in faith and asking you to consider your position, your role, and your life. We're asking you to radically evaluate your life and faith. We're asking for work in the name of God. It's almost too cliché to roll out a verse, but it's a necessity we need to glue to our lives.

You are the salt of the earth. But if the salt loses its saltiness, how can it be made salty again? It is no longer good for anything, except to be thrown out and trampled by men.

You are the light of the world. A city on a hill cannot be hidden. Neither do people light a lamp and put it under a bowl. Instead they put it on its stand, and it gives light to everyone in the house. In the same way, let your light shine before men, that they may see your good deeds and praise your Father in heaven. Let your light shine, so they can see your good deeds and praise the Father. We're advocating work: not speeches, not sermons, not four-hour weekend workshops. Just work.

MATTHEW 5:13-16

Dear children, let us not love with words or tongue but with actions and in truth.

1 JOHN 3:18

Matthew got it. John got it. Get up and do something. We don't care what it is. Just take some action. The rule should be "Do anything short of sin."

Give to the poor. Feed the hungry. Evangelize on a city street. Help a kid who has cancer. Join the fight against pornography. Share some time with the elderly. Love your neighbor. Play with and teach a little kid. Make yourself available to a teenager who needs a mentor. Fix someone's car. Paint a house. Talk to a homosexual about his or her faith. Pull a drunk out of the gutter, and give him something to eat. Give the homeless guy a place to crash. Bring a hooker to church. Spend the afternoon talking to an inmate at the local jail.

You get the idea. Bottom line: Get off your butt and do something.

1.6 JUST JUNKIES

J.R. and I consider ourselves reaction junkies. Not attention junkies. Please know that there's a big difference between the two. One says, "Please have something to say about what I'm saying or doing." The other says, "Please have something to say about me, my thoughts, my actions. Me … me … me."

Christ was a reaction junkie of a sort. As a result, he created the biggest reaction the world has ever seen.

We would love to say we are perfect examples of Christ. The truth is, the Enemy would love us to drive XXXchurch into the ground. He would love for us to crave the fame of our peers and say, "Oh, look at us! Traveling the country-side, getting people to react, just like Christ did. Aren't we great? Look at our big Web sites, look at our cool resources. Check out our five-part series and all the cool merchandising. Order today—we take credit cards!"

Satan does a great job ministering to those in the church who love the fame and power associated with helping others heal. You can get drunk on helping people change their lives. Unchecked, the lie becomes "God had little to do with it, and I am solely responsible for this new life." Believe the lie long enough and you start believing your own press. Satan then devours those seeking themselves by helping them celebrate their own self-centeredness. In the long run, the lie turns into a self-righteous theology that says, "I am the bottom line in the lives of people." The ministry quickly becomes about a man and what the man has to say or not say.

Satan teaches the self-centered and self-obsessed how to be what J.R. and I call "Born Again Lazy": how to actively fulfill selfish desires while keeping Christ at arm's length. Satan ultimately wants your reaction to be a call to do nothing for others. He's looking for you to say nothing, leave nothing, and offer nothing.

Jesus, on the other hand, seeks to mix it up. When Christ calls us, he engages our sin, not our dreams, goals, or passions. He died for our sins. He served humanity by giving his life. He's asking you to do the same. Grab the people around you and serve them.

Jesus understands the human drive to be important and valued by other people. He is here to set us free from ourselves. The freedom needs to express itself in selflessness and service to others. He's looking for your reaction to the world to be that of a servant.

1.7
HIS REACTION

Be in the world, not of the world. We love to screw this up. We automatically assume we should check out and pay no attention to the pop culture radar. Forget about the people who are led astray. Build a bunker in the backyard, cover the kids' eyes and ears, and hope all your willpower and energy will be enough for the world to stay away. The problem with this behavior is when you follow Christ, you will be asked to serve those who are of the world.

Then there are other Christians who take this in the opposite direction, focusing too much on pop culture, letting too much of the world come into their lives until they stop talking or thinking about Jesus altogether. Let's talk about *Lord of the Rings* or the latest episode of *Lost* instead.

When Jesus walked the earth, he created reaction by simply living a sinless life and fulfilling the will of the Father. How great it must have been to watch him in a crowd as he got in the grill of the religious leaders. He didn't argue; he didn't resist; he simply laid the truth of his life in front of them.

Think about the number of people who wanted to be near Jesus, to touch him, ask him questions, share a meal with him, and even go into business with him. Some of these people wanted nothing to do with God the Father; they just wanted to hang with the popularity of the moment.

Jesus didn't build a bunker, move to Waco, or even encourage others to get away from the craziness of the world they were living in. In fact, quite the opposite happened: He led his disciples to the cities and towns most likely to grab and kill them. And all along the way, he loved those who didn't have a clue as to what he was up to. Again, serving as he went, without the need to be stroked, accepted, or driven around in a Hummer.

Regardless of what his life looked like and how offensive his ministry was, Jesus continually told those around him to do two things: go and do. He healed people on the Sabbath. He was seen with prostitutes. He questioned authority. He ate with tax collectors, and he pulled lepers out of the gutter. The first time he preached, people tried to kill him. Finally, he did the unthinkable. He gave himself willingly to die for a bunch of ragtag, ungrateful sinners. He needed everyone around him to understand the value of love, which is action in other people's lives.

Do you honor his actions? Do you push the envelope for him? Is it important for you to express his life and his actions to the people around you? Are you working for him, or are you working for your own end? This question cannot be answered until we realize we all sin and fall short of his glory. Not my glory or your glory: God's.

Therefore, we are all the same. No need to bear the burden of terminal uniqueness. No need to think the next guy has it all together, because he doesn't. No one knows exactly what they are saying or doing, and if you find that person who claims or acts as if he's got it all together, I'll show you a person who does not have Christ in his heart.

A lot of what churches and pastors are doing today is seeking attention. Whether they are ministers with big or small congregations, they are driving for man's fame, not God's. You can see it twenty-four hours a day, seven days a week on Christian TV. You flip it on and *bam!* there it is: the needs of man, not the needs of God. From the need of money to the glory of personal treasure, it's all right there. It's a tightly held belief that our God is a give-and-get sort of fella, just waiting for you to give, so he can do his part to improve your life.

1.8 CHURCH DECAY

Too harsh? I don't think so. Hit Matthew 5. What are the unchurched seeing?

When will we stop buying and believing that God is okay with our not doing anything for his having faith in us and being our salvation? When will we admit our sin one to another and get on with salvation?

What J.R. and I are hearing is sort of a rally call. It's hard to go anywhere in Christian circles without encountering the "I want to start something new" conversation. People all over the country are starving for something new. The modern church has decided to feed on Value Meal Theology. The creativity of the Holy Spirit has stopped, because we are mass replicating two or three different messages a month for the consumption of the American spiritual appetite. Nothing new, nothing inspired, and nothing created in the name of Christ, just topics to help with happiness and recovery from our bad self-images or failing self-esteem. We have made the message series commonplace and tacked on Thorazine-loaded Bible studies to placate American Christian appetites until the next CD or DVD is on sale in the lobby.

Church decay is real, and the voices screaming, "Rebuild!" are getting louder. When was the last time you questioned what the church was doing to get the gospel into your community? When was the last time you stopped talking for an hour and just did something—anything—for someone other than yourself (and I'm not talking about being nice during the holidays)? I'm talking about the middle of summer, or while you were on vacation, or when you were in a hurry, or when it was so inconvenient that it hurt you to do it.

The voices that want to rebuild are not the voices that are screaming, "I am the greatest in the church!" The rebuilding voices sound like service. The Last Supper must have really bummed Jesus out. The brilliant disciples in all their wisdom argued about who was the greatest among them. They even took their squabble to Christ, who I'm sure had a lot on his mind. He looked at these guys who'd been with him some time and shook his head. "Listen," he said. "The one who serves is greatest."

1.9
HONEST LIKE A
GAY GUY

I was on a plane not too long ago, where I sat in front of an ex-homosexual. Yes, that's right, a real live gay man. Well ... ex-gay man. He was brilliantly honest. He laid out his story to the guy sitting next to him, and we all did everything we could to eavesdrop on this one.

Within minutes of hearing the ex-gay guy's testimony, our entire section of the plane knew more about him than his own mother did. He started out by telling the man sitting next to him, "I have problems, but so does everyone. I used to be very promiscuous. Not anymore." He was so confident. "Thank God I am no longer gay, but for a while I was. I was programmed that way. I'm convinced I was." By this time the back three rows of the plane were doing whatever they could to hear him. We couldn't wait for the next thing he was going say. It was better than any magazine or movie the airline could offer up.

The ex-gay guy went on to profess Jesus as his Lord and Savior. It was simply awesome. The guy next to him took it all in stride, a class act, never once turning away from him, always engaged and always ready for what was next, even asking questions as the story rolled out.

We couldn't decide who we were more proud of, the ex-gay guy or the dude sitting next to him.

The ex-gay guy let this stranger, as well as three other rows, into his life. He let his strengths and weaknesses see the light of day. He gave us all a reason to be humble and transparent to one another. He shined a light on rows 17, 18, and 19. A light the likes of which none of us had ever seen before. Who knows how many people were touched by that story. Who knows how many people stopped and chatted with God that day, because an ex-gay guy shared his testimony loud and clear with a stranger on a plane.

As we got off that plane, we let him walk by. I smiled and stared hard at him, trying to make a connection like, "Hey, buddy, we get it, we're not gay, but we love the Lord. Thanks for the story and the courage it took to let it go." He walked by. No smile, no nothing; just walked by. The rest of us looked at each other, knowing something wild had just happened. We will never forget his honesty and courage.

How I wished the entire church could have been on that plane. How I wished his honesty could be bottled and injected into every Christian in this country. The ex-gay guy broke our hearts. He made us scream out to God for our own weaknesses. He made us praise God that he was even in the world. He made us want more from God. Most of all, the guy reminded us of our desire to wear our stories on our sleeves and roll them out with as much class and grace as he did.

We wandered over to baggage claim, staring at our new ex-gay-guy hero. We were asking ourselves questions and understanding that this guy is the new church. He literally embodied what we, as disciples, need to be doing every minute of every day. I looked up as he grabbed his bag off the carousel. "Too bad the church will never give this guy a voice. Perhaps that's why he does so well on planes," I said as I watched him slip outside and into a taxi. "Good luck, ex-gay guy."

This whole encounter left me with questions: What happened to the admission of sin in the church? What happened to the idea that we are all sinners and that we must maintain accountability in our lives?

Jesus did his best to correct the disciples and their sin along the way, from Simon Peter, who the Lord called by two names depending on his actions, to Judas, who Christ had no problem calling out at the Last Supper. What's the example here? What about Paul giving it up in Galatians 6:1–10?

GALATIANS 6:1–10

Brothers, if someone is caught in a sin, you who are spiritual should restore him gently. But watch yourself, or you also may be tempted. Carry each other's burdens, and in this way you will fulfill the law of Christ. If anyone thinks he is something when he is nothing, he deceives himself. Each one should test his own actions. Then he can take pride in himself, without comparing himself to somebody else, for each one should carry his own load.

Anyone who receives instruction in the word must share all good things with his instructor.

Do not be deceived: God cannot be mocked. A man reaps what he sows. The one who sows to please his sinful nature, from that nature will reap destruction; the one who sows to please the Spirit, from the Spirit will reap eternal life. Let us not become weary in doing good, for at the proper time we will reap a harvest if we do not give up. Therefore, as we have opportunity, let us do good to all people, especially to those who belong to the family of believers.

Paul was killing them with the idea of confronting sin and letting people know it's okay to admit and be honest about their sin. He also lets us know that, if we have received the instruction and get it, we should help others get it. Not simply run in the other direction, hoping God will sort it all out.

God does depend on us for a few things. We are not to simply stand idly by and wait for divine instruction with every decision in our lives.

Christ sought out people. He picked them up, healed them, loved them, laughed with them, went to their depths and pulled them out, then died for them. Christ paid for humanity with his life. Don't let his sacrifice go another day in your life without your pulling someone up out of his or her sin and asking if you can help. Because the truth is, you can. Proverbs 28 is filled with reminders for approaching sin in your life as well as the lives of others. Verse 13 says, "He who conceals his sins does not prosper, but whoever confesses and renounces them finds mercy." Fast-forward to verse 23: "He who rebukes a man will in the end gain more favor than he who has a flattering tongue."

1.10
HONESTLY
DOING

Honestly, what are you doing? Are you and your church focused on destroying sin, or are you more concerned about your church's appearance?

J.R. and I have this thing about honesty. We believe the biggest problem with Christians isn't about filling the pews or worrying about the next big series campaign. Honesty—that's the church's number one struggle. From the tender of the flock to the flock itself, we couldn't tell the truth to save our souls. The church has convinced itself that truth is a commodity of salvation and not the author of it. We are so busy building a process for honest conversations that we have lost the ability to stand up and say, "I've got a problem with sin!" We have stifled confession to save embarrassment.

We have taken pride to new levels, and along the climb, we've decided anyone with a sin problem is better left to fend for himself or herself. Funny—as I write this, I can hear the critics saying that we are misguided and disillusioned. The problem is, confession comes very slowly to the American church. We are only honest when we get caught: when our marriage is suddenly on the rocks, when our kids are in trouble, when our career takes a turn, or when we just can't go on.

We are so consumed with hiding from our honesty that we have decided it's okay to ignore it. As a result, we leave the honesty and its accompanying sin lying in the aisles, hoping the janitor will sweep it away as we close the doors to the public, plug our ears, close our eyes, and hope God somehow sorts it all out.

While we are doing our best to ignore sin, throughout the week, our neighbors are peering into our lives, scoffing at us, the Sunday morning hypocrites who live across the street or down the block. Why should they follow our example when we are ignoring Christ in our own lives?

The honesty problem is exhausting. We hide in Christian self-righteousness while leading others to live comfortable lives as Born Again Lazy. We have stopped following Christ as Savior and positioned him as a happy, feel-good philosopher who works on Sundays but doesn't bother us during the week while we're living a lazy lifestyle. The problem here is that Christ doesn't offer deals for salvation. *It is what it is*. Christ died for you. He died a horrible death on a cross so you can have salvation. This isn't about your dreams, plans, or designs—this is about what he did for you. Honesty has been replaced by our needs for fulfilled dreams, passions, and minute-to-minute wants.

Paul was completely honest in Romans 7. It's almost too painful to read as he lays out his life. The church seems to miss this chapter, and J.R. and I do, too, at times. But, man, do we get it, because we are so much like Paul: human and born of sin.

ROMANS
7:14-20
We know that the law is spiritual; but I am unspiritual, sold as a slave to sin. I do not understand what I do. For what I want to do I do not do, but what I hate I do. And if I do what I do not want to do, I agree that the law is good. As it is, it is no longer I myself who do it, but it is sin living in me. I know that nothing good lives in me, that is, in my sinful nature. For I have the desire to do what is good, but I cannot carry it out. For what I do is

not the good I want to do; no, the evil I do not want to do—this I keep on doing. Now if I do what I do not want to do, it is no longer I who do it, but it is sin living in me that does it.

It is Paul's candor, his honesty, that frees him from sin. God only knows what Paul was up to. I know what we are capable of doing. The sky's the limit on the amount of pain and confusion we can create in our lives and the lives of others.

The one thing that will always land us on our knees is honesty. It usually happens when we are out of excuses, out of promises, out of outs. We quickly hit the floor and scream out in pain for God to help us as we admit the sin in our lives. He will answer those prayers. But his Word is also clear that we need to admit our sin to each other. This is where we will find the freedom from our sin, not in a dark room filled with those screaming, isolated, honest moments of prayer.

Is any one of you in trouble? He should pray. Is anyone happy? Let him sing songs of praise. Is any one of you sick? He should call the elders of the church to pray over him and anoint him with oil in the name of the Lord. And the prayer offered in faith will make the sick person well; the Lord will raise him up. If he has sinned, he will be forgiven. Therefore confess your sins to each other and pray for each other so that you may be healed. The prayer of a righteous man is powerful and effective.

JAMES 5:13-16

We can't miss this. Honesty is a part of the prayer equation. Honesty among each other is vital to healing.

Should you decide to follow Christ, you're looking at blood, sweat, and tears. Peace and happiness are by-products, but you have to work it. Simon Peter was told to back off when Christ rebuked him for messing with Christ's eternal mission. It must have stunk. Imagine your Lord and Savior in your grill, saying, "Get behind me, Satan!" God's Son calling you out? It must have been

one of the worst moments in Simon Peter's life. But the rebuke offered Peter the truth he needed. Jesus didn't sit him down, call five
people, start a recovery group, put up a Web site with an 800
number.... No, he simply applied the truth directly to Peter's life.
Jesus turned and said to Peter, "Get behind me, Satan! You are a
stumbling block to me. You do not have in mind the things of
God, but the things of men."

Peter probably stood and stared at Jesus. Can you imagine
what a failure he must have thought he was? I would have died
right there. I think Peter most likely did. Jesus goes on to say,

MARK 8:34-38 *If anyone would come after me, he must deny himself
and take up his cross and follow me. For whoever wants
to save his life will lose it, but whoever loses his life for
me and for the gospel will save it. What good is it for a
man to gain the whole world, yet forfeit his soul? Or
what can a man give in exchange for his soul? If anyone
is ashamed of me and my words in this adulterous and
sinful generation, the Son of Man will be ashamed of
him when he comes in his Father's glory with the holy
angels.*

God is saying the same thing to the church today. Get your
head wrapped around me and not around your own fame. Take
your face off the posters, the CDs, the DVDs, the books, and
marketing collateral. Get ahold of yourselves. Stop with the all-
inclusive meetings with pastors, stop building the perfect leader,
and give me your attention. Fall flat. Admit your sin as a church,
one to another. Tend, not talk.

CHAPTER 2
BORN AGAIN LAZY

CH 2 | BORN AGAIN LAZY

Do not merely listen to the word, and so deceive your- JAMES 1:22-25
selves. Do what it says. Anyone who listens to the word
but does not do what it says is like a man who looks at
his face in a mirror and, after looking at himself, goes
away and immediately forgets what he looks like. But
the man who looks intently into the perfect law that
gives freedom, and continues to do this, not forgetting
what he has heard, but doing it—he will be blessed in
what he does.

James understood one big thing about Christians: We love to talk, but we don't necessarily like to get up, out, and get it done. It's one thing to proclaim Christ on Sunday morning; it's another to get wrapped up in your next-door neighbor's life on any given day and ask about his or her faith.

James knew we would find things other than Christ to consume our lives. He knew how hard it would be to step up for Jesus and simply walk in faith. The book of James was made for people like J.R. and me. We were the very definition of *Born Again Lazy*.

Born Again Laziness is common among Christians today. They fill the seats of both megachurches and small-town fellowships. There's inaction, idle worship, and a tendency to stay exclusive as a fellowship and not go beyond the parking lot. As a church, we have become Born Again Lazy. Lazy with outreach, lazy with money, lazy with our families, lazy with prayer, lazy with fasting, lazy with studying God's Word, lazy with him.

Lazy with the lost.

It may be sin we don't see, or it may be a glaring defect that stops us from exercising our faith. Either way, we are creating Christians whose main desire is to please themselves. We have stopped confronting sin and helping the lost, exchanging them for comfortable conversations and happy moments, all in the name of not offending. From feel-good sermons to give-and-get messages, today's pulpits look more like the set of *Dr. Phil* than the resting place for the weary. We focus solely on individual achievement and happiness—never mind the sick, the lost, the unchurched. We wind up hoping they find our building through the MapQuest link on the church Web site. We gather in circles and pray, "Bring them, Lord," without ever realizing that we can just go get 'em.

2.1
J.R. THE LAZY

The beer is going down easy; the cigarettes I'm smoking are being tossed in the bush next to me. I am loud, funny, irresponsibly the center of attention. I am a self-proclaimed born-again Christian. I am a walking disaster before God. My career is great, my staff loves me, and I have the ear of my colleagues. It is the end of a long day ... why shouldn't a disciple of Christ get lit?

The combination of booze and the Holy Spirit is like a sledgehammer wrapped in soft velvet. I have become that guy. "Born Again Lazy." Heartfelt, well intentioned, lost like Judas. Thinking only of myself, bent on my own plans and designs.

Covering my sin is calculated. I tell lies about my relationship with God, hoping people still place stock in me. "The Lord's doing a work in me," I'll say. "The Lord tells me I'm okay right where I am," is another one. "In God's time." "I'm in God's waiting room." "The Word really isn't clear about that." I have a whole list. I have become saved in sin.

I am driving, praying I won't get stopped by the cops. I am guilty for actions, words, knowledge of the truth. It hurts as I think about how people count on me. I pray my drunken wandering will take me safely into my driveway.

The stones under my feet crunch as I make my way from the car to the deck. The house is dark, it's late, my wife, Di, is asleep. I have killed her spirit over the last three years. She has taken a backseat to my sin. I could spend eternity apologizing for things I've said and done, and it wouldn't be enough.

The Holy Spirit screams at me as the key drives into the door, *What are you doing?*

At least I'm honest in replying: *I'm ignoring the truth, that's what I'm doing! Leave me alone!* It's hard enough sober. Drunk should be hallowed ground for a guy like me.

The bed feels good; I have stopped caring. I stare at the ceiling until I am mindless.... I drift asleep. No prayer, no hope, no freedom. Born Again Lazy.

**2.2
TERMINAL
UNIQUENESS**

You would think these behaviors rest solely with someone who doesn't know Christ; unfortunately, Christ is all too familiar with wandering sheep. All too familiar with the Born Again Lazy. The truth? Our sinful behavior has occupied most of our salvation. Fallen man ... there's nothing like it. We slowly became our own god out of sinful necessity. We covered the truth with everything socially acceptable and justified our shabby Christianity with "Oprahology." We gave the Lord only a portion of our lives—the portion that didn't need commitment. We built our houses on sand and reaped the rewards of tragic begging.

J.R. and I would come to understand that we *wanted* to love Christ. We even asked him, *Lord, what will you have us do?* The answer we each got was straight out of Matthew 19.

Answer: Sell it all, come follow me.

Translation for our lives: Put everything in front of me and leave it all.

Our Christian answer back: No thanks.

The crazy part of the equation, though, is that Jesus didn't chase us down; he didn't write us e-mails extending yet another invitation over and over and over again. He was cool with our answer and moved on to other things. The rich young ruler in Matthew 19 had done all Jesus had said for him to do, except the one thing that was a deal breaker, and Jesus knew it. He asked the rich young ruler to give up what made him, him: money. The rich young ruler went away sorrowful, bummed out that he couldn't do it. Imagine the Son of God in your grill, telling you, "You can be with me forever if you ..." and you look at him and walk. We did.

And for years we thought we were justified, because we went to church, knew the lingo, dropped a twenty in the basket, prayed for people, blah, blah, blah. Truth is, we were no closer to the King than we were the day before we heard his voice for the first time. We had become Born Again Lazy.

2.3 EVERYONE ELSE EXCEPT J.R.

In the spring of my eternal drunkenness, Di and I moved to Cleveland. I was a self-obsessed TV producer and Christian hypocrite. Hired as an executive producer for a local television station, off I went.

It was my job to (a) make people watch TV and (b) manage the zoo that is the American newsroom. I'd been a Christian for many years but had only been pretending to live the life; I'd really been living for myself, which led to many hidden sins.

TV supplied a wonderful environment for me to justify my sin, and I was way too happy to argue about why God had planted me in this environment. I mean, I was witnessing to a lost and dying generation all in the name of television, drunkenness, and good Christian living. What could be better? I was living on both sides of the fence.

As the early weeks rolled out on our Cleveland tenure, God's voice became increasingly louder, taking the form of some great radio preachers I would listen to in the car, driving to and from work. I could not escape sentences like "Take up the cross and follow me," and "Lose your life and you will find it." I was scared, but I told no one. The truth was, I knew my TV career was over; I knew God was calling me to leave that industry. I knew I was Born Again Lazy. The Bible is filled with people like me: people who heard God's voice and ignored it.

God had been pounding on me for years about my salvation. Calling me to leave my life and follow him. And I truly thought I'd been doing just that. I had accepted Christ when I was eighteen, read the Bible, gone to church, helped others, witnessed, had the lingo down. But the pounding of God's hand and the sound of his voice never stopped. I was the perfect American Christian, sitting in the mire of the Sunday-to-Sunday existence. No prayer, no study, and no interaction with the lost or unchurched. I *was* the lost. I *was* the unchurched. My sin kept my butt in the pew and my head wondering what the next drink special was at happy hour on Friday.

Sunday mornings, I'd be up for church and out the door by nine o'clock, a smile on my face. I'd get there, sing a little, listen a little, pray a little, ignore the ushers as they passed the basket, act as if I didn't see the guy behind me trying to say hi during that awkward "greeting time." I'd smile at my wife as our eyes caught each other's during worship and wonder if she was into it. It looked like she was, so I looked like I was.

I was a great spiritual leader. After service came the mad dash to the car, where I flipped on the radio to distract from conversation about God and the lack of my relationship with him and my family. By the time we hit the first stoplight, inevitably I would start tearing down the pastor's message. I'd get through the door of our house by noon, hit the couch by 12:10, and have the whole rest of the day to immerse myself in sin.

The most amazing part of my Sundays? There was a guy who kept attendance at the church. I would see him counting the people from the balcony from time to time. I'm pretty sure he included me as one of the people in the pews. Me! I had nothing to do with that place, and he still counted me.

The Lord was calling me out. I hear a lot of people say "in God's time." That's crap, plain and simple. God isn't a mailman, and he isn't Santa. If we're waiting for him, we are placing all the responsibility squarely on him, but he needs *us* to get up and out, not *God* up and out. God did his part, in the form of the cross, and it's our responsibility to carry that message of love to all the nations ... now! Not when things seem to work out better for us, or when we have more money or more time, or when the kids have gone to college, or when we find a mate, or when we get married, or when the new job comes or ... or ... or ... or ...

Now.

Time was ticking for me. It's funny how we put time on God, as if he has some kind of spiritual Rolex up there. We expect things to happen for us, so we pray and wait, wait and pray. Then when it becomes painfully obvious that it ain't happening, we pray again and scream, "What are you doing, God? Help me, God! Please help me!" We even work ourselves into doubt and, from there, occasionally start to resent God.

His time for us is now. Right now.

**2.4
GOD'S TIME**

Being Born Again Lazy oftentimes means we are in a comfortable stage of waiting. Not too long ago, a guy e-mailed me and told me he was in God's waiting room, waiting for God to tell him his next move. I wrote back and asked if he had to schedule an appointment for this visit.

He wrote back very sincerely and said he'd just obtained his college degree, but this waiting room thing prevented him from doing anything with it. He told me he was landscaping while he was waiting to hear from God. At the time of his e-mail, he was newly married, with a child on the way. Here's a piece of advice for the single women out there: If you meet a guy who tells you he's in God's waiting room and he wants to date you or marry you, tell him the wait will be a lonely one, 'cause you're not interested. This well-intentioned guy had bought one big lie about being a Christian; he worked himself into a hole, thinking God had something new for him other than what was going on inside the Bible.

God forbid I say it, but if you're looking for what God wants you to do, it's in the Bible. Yeah, it might get a little boring as you first start investigating it, but it's right there in black and white ... and red. It's really that easy. Regardless of what happened with this young man, we must help one another understand that the Word of God is clear about what to do and when to do it. *Now* is when, and the what is easy: It's called "anything but wait."

So the big problem with being Born Again Lazy is God's time, because his time is now, and we generally think change has to happen over time. As Christians, we are fond of prolonging the inevitable, seeking ourselves right into ignoring God and his Word. When God called the disciples, they didn't take a class or have a five-hour talk with a counselor. They went. They left their lives, everything. It must have been the toughest thing they had ever done. J.R. and I often say there's no way we could have done it, except for one thing: We have! It just took us longer to get it going, and now that we are here, it's a riot.

2.5 SPIRITUAL VOMIT

God's voice was becoming louder with every drink, every smoke, every hurtful thing I did to my wife, every foul word uttered out of my disrespectful mouth. I was dying. Nothing seemed to matter: my relationships, my thoughts, philosophies, theologies—nothing. I was screaming at God, "What is going on? Please help me! Show me what to do!" I was sincerely asking God for these things, but I was still willing to suffer the pain of my sin and not change. No study of the Word, no interaction, no counsel. I was hoping there was a prayer switch. I thought if I prayed really passionately, God would flip the switch and relieve me from all my sin.

It doesn't work that way. You must take the lead on change. God will not simply provide you relief unless he knows you are ready to immerse your life in him. That should have been my prayer: *Lord, give me wisdom to change.*

I was angry, and my wife took the brunt of it. I abused her verbally; my words were harsh, filled with criticism and venom. To this day I am not sure how she survived me, other than God's loving arms wrapped around her. Anything would set me off: from the way she would say something, to not understanding me when I talked. I would yell, scream, rant for long periods of time. I would go on at length about how stupid she was and how she was constantly missing the point. I forced her to listen and look at me while I screamed at her. Many times she would burst into tears, and I wouldn't care. I was her own personal hell for a number of years. My justification for that behavior was simple: I had a crap family growing up, and I had a lot of pressure at the job. Those were the facts, but the facts often have little to do with the truth. And the truth was that I was a Christian man ignoring God's call. I was Born Again Lazy.

Di stuck it out with me. I knew she was parrying my assaults and reading the Word. I could feel the power of God all around her, and quite frankly, I was pissed. I resented her discipline. I resented her spiritual leadership at the expense of my shabby leadership. I would walk by her in the morning as she was reading the Bible, and I would get pissed. My sin would make me recoil at the very sight of her and her little Mother Teresa moments. The truth in her life was making me so uncomfortable that I did my best to avoid it. Conversations about God or the Bible would be thrown to the side to make room for my rants and crazy, off-the-wall views of Christ and his followers. I was a walking disaster. Born Again Lazy.

I became the rich young ruler: "I'm doing everything right, so let's have it, Jesus." Except Christ knew what I was doing. He knew where my heart was and challenged me. He told the rich young ruler to sell it all, give it to the poor, and follow him. In a split second, Jesus tore up that guy's life. The ruler was attached to cash; I was attached to booze and lying. The rich young ruler walked away knowing his alliance to money was more important than his alliance to the kingdom of God. The Bible says he was sorrowful. Translation: He was torn up and deflated.

Sometimes I think about him, and I hope his heart was softened before his death. It sucked, frankly. Picture me living day to day with a head full of Christ and a heart full of sin. A wannabe disciple. Telling the world how great it was to be me, while falling to sin's slow and painful death. Sometimes it came in the form of booze, pride, and poor leadership inside the family. Whatever the infraction, it was one of the classic signs of being Born Again Lazy. It had to be cleaned up; it had to change. I had to change.

If anyone considers himself religious and yet does not keep a tight rein on his tongue, he deceives himself and his religion is worthless. Religion that God our Father accepts as pure and faultless is this: to look after orphans and widows in their distress and to keep oneself from being polluted by the world.

JAMES 1:26-27

The world is all too happy to recognize talent and pour out praise and adulation among people, and we, in return, are thrilled to accept the plaques and honors, while yelling, "I know I'm great! I'm so awesome! Look at me, me, me, and me. You people should see what I'm gonna do next!" We eat that stuff up and are dying from sin.

2.6
THE
APPEARANCE

As we travel, we hear a lot of things from a lot of people:

"I am a good Christian."

"I go to church."

"I volunteer."

"I pray, read the Bible."

"I am a good husband/wife."

"My kids are great."

"I have good friends."

"I don't need to be that committed or a disciple or a missionary to love God."

"We do what we do for God; you do what you do."

For years, Christians have created excuses to justify living like lazy followers of Christ. We come up with some pretty distorted arguments for not pursuing a higher relationship with God. One truth about being Born Again Lazy is that the *world* loves how it looks—it looks good.

The world sees people who go to church living fully

functioning lives, making money, having relationships, getting it done—and everyone has a big, toothy grin doing it. It does look good. What we really need to show the world is life-changing functionality. We need to mirror Christ in all of our activities. This doesn't mean we wear robes, travel with a bunch of ragtag crazies, speak differently, and live poor. It means we come clean about the sin in our lives and live out our lives in faith.

So what's the big deal? The big deal is the inaction. James tells us to help the widows and orphans. Translation: Get up and out and help people. We have become consumed with what faith looks like instead of what it is doing. God says the religion he wants comes in the form of helping people, not playacting with flat, empty, good-looking smiles filled with selfish desire, wrapped around nothing to say or do. He needs us in the trenches, thinking about others and leading them to Christ.

2.7
LEAVING LAZY

For me, Lazy started shaking itself off once I started to see the fruit of my labor, or the lack thereof. Some trees can yield some ugly, funky fruit, and that's what happened to me. One day I woke up, looked at my life, and saw a giant hole that had been created from selfish, self-centered propaganda, from living a life controlled by whims and feelings and not God's perfect will for me or my wife. That day, though it was great and changed my life forever, was hard, to say the least. Frankly, it sucked. It sucked because what it meant was a good shot of honesty, which usually comes from someone you love. The kind of honesty that takes you out at the knees. The kind of reality you want to run from. The kind of wake-up call you argue with until all the words run together, and you even hear your own crap coming back to you. It's a literal come-to-Jesus conversation.

For me it was when my wife looked at me one morning and said, "J.R., I'm leaving if you continue to drink." As those words were still coming out of her mouth, I was trying to plan around her anxiety. I thought, *Maybe I will just drink less, maybe I will just not drink around her, and maybe I can just drink on Fridays.* I didn't want to hear the pain, the devastation caused by my being Born Again Lazy. I only heard my voice justifying the sin I had let loose in my life.

One massive thing took place that day that forever changed my life, and I continue to tell people: My wife mirrored my behavior. She called my sin out, which is exactly what needed to happen. She didn't let me sit on it, she didn't kowtow to my craziness—she came with both barrels loaded and said, "This is it! Either you deal with it or I will."

I did, thank God. It had little to do with drinking; this was about falling flat at the Lord's feet and admitting defeat in my sin. This was about no longer being Born Again Lazy.

2.8
THE OTHER
SIDE OF LAZY

We are geared to think that addictions, compulsions, or other crazy brain things we were born with are to blame for our weaknesses and bad behavior. But being Born Again Lazy is all about *you*, the ego, a head full of "truth," and a heart brewing with rebellion. This is squarely about *your* sin, not your ancestors', creating division between you and God. You can name any sin you would like, and we will steer you right to the cross. The disciples faced walking away after Christ was crucified; Paul even admitted he did the things he did not want to do. We are not unique; we are simply born of sin. And once we recognize that it's in every area of our lives, we step into faith and away from being Born Again Lazy. We must know the truth and exercise it in faith. Which means we will get off our butts, tell the truth about ourselves to those around us, and plan a life around Christ and all that he stands for.

What good is it, my brothers, if a man claims to have faith but has no deeds? Can such faith save him?

JAMES 2:14

James hits it out of the park here. He asks you a question: Can you have a faith that saves you outside of deeds? Well? We say no. As a result of living our lives devoid of deeds, of doing things for others, we left ourselves spiritually paralyzed. We had nothing to do, nothing to say.

J.R. and I struggle daily with small concepts about faith, but the one we can hold on to is this one from James: do. Just do. *Deeds* equal "your getting completely out of yourself," and when you step up into another's life, you are fulfilling a law of Christ.

The church must grab ahold of this. We must force ourselves to understand living beyond ourselves every day. Deeds will connect us to one another and cement us to God's will.

What does the other side of Lazy look like? It looks great. There is no need to put on airs, and honesty becomes the norm of conversation. Faith becomes your daily exercise. Words like *peace, happiness,* and *fulfillment* actually mean something. The long term is the most exciting part of the faith: the ability to truly know yourself. This means better decision making in the name of Christ. We so often struggle with decisions. We ask, *Is this what God wants?* The majority of us struggle with, *Am I making the right choice?* We must embrace the Word of God as *the* practical source of "truth and knowledge" to apply to our lives, not just a study guide or something we whip out on Sundays. Not being Lazy means we read a little and implement a lot.

2.9
THE DAY TO
DAY

J.R. and I have a routine. Routine wraps itself in action. The first established routine for us is prayer, twice a day, on our knees, no matter what. From there, it's maintenance praying for the rest of the day.

We also make a daily habit of putting the Bible in our lives. This is as simple as reading James and finding something to do. We suggest reading the Bible in twos every day: Read two pages or two verses or two books, or read one verse in the New Testament and one verse in the Old. Two by two. Do at least two every day. Don't let the Bible intimidate your everyday routine. It's been around for a long time, and you have a lifetime with it, so relax and read two.

Whether it's in the morning or at night (or both), let the discernment of the Holy Spirit be your two-guide.

J.R. and I also tell on ourselves. We seek accountability with people around us. We let others know what we are thinking and doing. The Bible calls it *confession*. We call it *having the guts to be honest with the people around you*. Find that one person you can share your life with and let it out. And know one thing: Everyone around you is still figuring it out too. The people who look as if they are the most together are most likely the people who need to read this chapter. So confess, often, face-to-face.

The last thing to keep you in routine and away from being Born Again Lazy is simply to get connected with the lost and unchurched around you. Challenge yourself to talk to others about faith, about why people don't believe, about why you doubt. Talk about the history you have with God and what that means in your life and your family's life. Create relationships around you. Your unsaved neighbors are just like you, and we'd be willing to bet that they are just as curious about you as you are about them. After all, don't you find yourself wondering what they're doing over there? Well, go find out.

It is hard to think we can live this disciplined life and actually maintain it. J.R. and I find ourselves struggling daily. We doubt, we justify, we still get rebellious. We even cuss from time to time. But—and this is a big but—we have a great handle on who we are. We have a good handle on how we react to things in our lives. We understand what happens when we feel that we want to run and take that spiritual vacation. We understand what happens inside of our anger or happiness.

How? All this understanding has come from hours of prayer, study, and putting ourselves out into a world that really needs Christ. We are not perfect, and if you want to know the truth about us, just ask our wives—they will give you details.

All the understanding about yourself still will not take

the place of one big thing, and that is the absolute truth of Christ in your life. You must understand that he is your Savior, and he is in charge. From there, getting rid of Born Again Laziness means you become responsible for your thoughts and behavior. Let's not back-burner the sin anymore; let's get it out and start living beyond ourselves, because we can.

That quiet little voice in your head telling you it's time for a change is the Holy Spirit. But *listening to* and *acting on* that voice are two different things. Don't wait for a lightning bolt to hit you or for that bush to start burning (although if that happens, I'd say it's definitely time). You need to place yourself in a solid position to act out your faith. Hear his voice and just step out. It's okay to start small, as long as you start, and stop being Lazy.

CHAPTER

OFFEND LIKE JESUS

3

CH 3 | OFFEND LIKE JESUS

All the people in the synagogue were furious when
they heard this. They got up, drove him out of the
town, and took him to the brow of the hill on which
the town was built, in order to throw him down the
cliff. But he walked right through the crowd and
went on his way.

LUKE 4:28-30

Craig and I are sitting at Limoncello, the best Italian restaurant that Boston's North End has to offer. The only bad thing about the place is that our wives aren't with us, which forces us to stare at each other's mugs while the exceptionally attentive wait staff caters to our every whim. The appetizers are great, the bread freshly baked and warm. The butter has a hint of garlic, and Gross is buying.

3.1
THE RANT

The main course at Limoncello is great, and the conversation turns to what we call "The Rant." The Rant sounds just like your rants, complaints, or general misgivings. It starts with something someone did or said. In our case, it's usually a Christian or someone tied closely to porn and Christ. We inevitably ask, "Why are Christians so overtly opinioned about everything?" One sentence always seems to make it into The Rant: "Why is the 'I'm offended' card used so often by the born-again Christian?"

As a faith, it seems Christians are doing two things: We are either offending people away from Christ with hypocrite rhetoric, or we are offending the very nature of sin with truth, which leads people to the cross.

In the interest of complete disclosure, J.R. and I run the day-to-day affairs of XXXchurch.com, an antiporn ministry dedicated to bringing awareness of the issues surrounding pornography. We do outreaches at porn shows, help people in the porn industry find their way out, and run the largest resource Web site for those struggling with porn.

3.2
TRUTHFUL
OFFENSE

For us, offense comes in the form of truth. We make no apologies for letting the general public know about the effects of sexual immorality. Paul, James, Luke, Mark, and countless others who have followed in their footsteps all dealt with the truth and its ability to set us free from sin. Their evangelizing tactics differed from one another, yet what they said and how they said it was so offensive to the world that most of them wound up dead at the hands of another man or country. We, thank God, do not have to worry about death for our beliefs in this country. Not yet anyway.

Every day J.R. and I come face-to-face with a sin so destructive that the only way to deal with it is to cut it off at the knees. That means we do radical outreaches away from mainstream Christianity. We want to speak directly to those wrapped up in sin. We want them to know, face-to-face, Christ is the answer.

We have been accused of being everything from publicity whores to false teachers. The one label we constantly get is "offensive." I'd say about 99 percent of those using that label are Christians—not my lost neighbor or the unchurched guy down the street, but the WWJD-bracelet-wearing, toothy-grinned Christian.

We are absolutely convinced that most Christians do not study the Bible. The gospel and its overt messages of selfless love and personal sacrifice seem to be lost on us. If the church were to openly teach or study the first five chapters of the book of Matthew, we would have more social unrest than France. There is more for people to argue about and get offended about and go nuts over in those first five chapters than our entire little antiporn ministry could ever dish out.

J.R. and I are putting the issue of offense concerning Christ and the world squarely in the lap of Christians. Not the world. Don't be offended by the world. Just turn off MTV. Stop buying the porn. Don't have that third drink. Stop sleeping with your neighbor's wife. Don't give the old lady in the car next to you the bird. Be willing to fight the good fight every day. This doesn't mean we match wits with the world. It means we are to be salt and light, to let the world see our good deeds so they, the world, can praise the Father. We collectively need to offend the senses of the world with the truth. The life of Christ was, is, and always will be offensive to the world.

One big thing to realize about people is that we all have that common desire to fill the hole that sin has created in our lives. We are all walking toward God, and along the way we must deal with sin. In all cases, the truth in people's lives will be offensive. Dealing with issues of pride, addiction, (name your sin here) will be a hard pill to swallow. We are flawed from the very start.

This is a tough concept for people to absorb, whether they know Christ or not. Remember your own history, and let that be your guide as you engage the world and all its craziness.

Sometimes I think we have lost our nerve as followers of Christ. I often think if we lived under the threat of death in this country, similar to what the early church faced, we would be on our game. The early church knew what the deal was. They knew it was only a matter of time before they were going to be put in jail and crucified. Paul called himself a prisoner of Christ. The first time I read that, I thought, *That ain't for me.* Think about it: Their message was so disturbing, so offensive, that they knew it meant death. When Jesus told his disciples, "Take up your cross and follow me," he was not talking about some little mission or job; he was talking about dying for the cause.

If you were faced with that, wouldn't you run? I have in the past, and at times I still do. We must understand that we have what we have because they did what they did. Every time you feel that thing in the center of your being when you think about God, you can thank a disciple or apostle who was willing to offend the senses of the world with the truth about Christ. I get bummed thinking about it. The American Christian will never know what that looks like in practice.

Truth will cause division. Truth offends. Christ laid it down fairly definitively in Matthew.

Do not suppose that I have come to bring peace to the earth. I did not come to bring peace, but a

MATTHEW
10:34-39

sword. For I have come to turn
"a man against his father,
a daughter against her mother,
a daughter-in-law against her mother-in-law—
a man's enemies will be the members of his own
household."

Anyone who loves his father or mother more than
me is not worthy of me; anyone who loves his son or
daughter more than me is not worthy of me; and any-
one who does not take his cross and follow me is not
worthy of me. Whoever finds his life will lose it, and
whoever loses his life for my sake will find it.

We are very blessed to have this faith in the United States, but we have grown soft on the truth. The church has made certain subjects, places, and people offensive, and as a result, we do not talk about the offense. Or if we do, we condemn it in the name of Christ. Worldly offense can bear itself out in resentment, anger, and pride. It's sin. We rarely dive into the Word to deal with offense, instead preferring to bury it, hide it, run from it, and in extreme cases, protest or picket it.

As Christians, we ultimately look at our kids and scream back to the world, which couldn't care less; and we say, "Look at what you're doing to the kids!" as if they will suddenly have a moment and completely stop what they are doing. Offense must be met with truth, not with crazy, half-cocked personal opinions about what is right and what is wrong.

The word *offense* has become *the* adjective that is used to define present-day Christianity. Offense has become a movement. We are not engaging truth with offense, we are using offense as a divining rod to find any given social problem and attack it. We look for the offense. We scrounge Scripture for its righteousness opposite, and off we go, e-mailing, calling, yelling, getting on TV, and basically letting the world know we're not gonna take it. What a lovely picture we have painted for those looking for God.

The world has come to identify us by what we hate and what we are offended by, instead of by what we love or why we love. We are the offensive ones. Are we offending away from Christ or offending toward him?

Jesus said to them, "I tell you the truth, unless you JOHN 6:53-66
eat the flesh of the Son of Man and drink his blood,
you have no life in you. Whoever eats my flesh and
drinks my blood has eternal life, and I will raise him
up at the last day. For my flesh is real food and my
blood is real drink. Whoever eats my flesh and drinks
my blood remains in me, and I in him. Just as the liv-
ing Father sent me and I live because of the Father,
so the one who feeds on me will live because of me.
This is the bread that came down from heaven. Your
forefathers ate manna and died, but he who feeds on
this bread will live forever." He said this while teach-
ing in the synagogue in Capernaum.

On hearing it, many of his disciples said, "This is a
hard teaching. Who can accept it?"

Aware that his disciples were grumbling about
this, Jesus said to them, "Does this offend you?
What if you see the Son of Man ascend to where he
was before! The Spirit gives life; the flesh counts for
nothing. The words I have spoken to you are spirit
and they are life. Yet there are some of you who do
not believe." For Jesus had known from the begin-
ning which of them did not believe and who would
betray him. He went on to say, "This is why I told you
that no one can come to me unless the Father has
enabled him."

From this time many of his disciples turned back
and no longer followed him.

Christ knew what he was doing as his life unfolded. As a kid, he taught in the synagogues. His mother and father worried about him. He fasted for forty days. He questioned religious leaders, even calling them children of the Devil. He healed people on the Sabbath, ate with sinners, raised people from the dead. He pulled an adulterous woman from the dirt and saved her from certain death. He turned the world upside down. He offended a sinful world with the truth.

3.3
OFFEND LIKE A
GUY NAMED
DAVE

I was eighteen when I heard Jesus call me. I was a mangled, sinful, pride-ridden, defensive punk. In late February 1985, I found myself in a kitchen with a guy named Dave. Dave wanted to know what I thought about God. I was too happy to tell him. "God sucks," I said with a grin ear to ear. I was hoping to get this guy going, make him mad by taking a shot at his God. It made all the sense in the world to me.

But he stayed calm. He didn't look away. He didn't want to hit me or yell at me. He stayed calm. I was amazed. He walked me to Christ. He said things like "God loves you" and "God will help you" and "God will change your life." I knew deep in my soul Dave was right, but I also knew I wanted nothing to do with it. Being God-Guy or believing in God would mean I had to change. It meant I was going to have to stop drinking, smoking, doing drugs, having sex. I was not down with that. I was miserably happy and content to live my life out in sin.

Dave got in my grill and loved me enough to offend my senses with the truth of Christ. He told me I was dangerously close to losing my life. He went on to say my life and what I had made of it sucked. His actual words were "A life away from God sucks." I knew he was right, and it pissed me off.

I sat in that kitchen, upset at this guy telling me about my life. *Who are you?* I thought. I really wanted to smack him in the face. He was right, and I wanted to run. I wanted to stop him as he went on exposing everything I had made of myself, every hurt, every illegal and shameful thing I had done. Every sin that made me, me. How did he know all this stuff?

Something started to happen to me. His words were cracking me open. My sin was all over that kitchen. He spoke nothing but truth about my life and what it had become. This guy didn't know me from Adam. I had met him at school, spoken a few words to him in passing, and somehow I'd wound up in this kitchen getting the crap kicked out of me.

Sometime during the conversation, Dave bowed his head and said, "Pray with me?" I laughed out loud, my last-ditch effort to make him upset, but he wasn't buying it. "God," he said in a loud, strong voice. His eyes were closed, head down.

I was like, "What are you doing?"

"Please help J.R.," he continued. "Help him see his life. Please help him to stop the things he is doing. Please let him see that the God I believe in loves him." Then Dave said, "Repeat after me, J.R."

Come on! "This is nuts," I said.

Dave didn't bat an eye. He just kept going. I was so uncomfortable I could barely stand it, so I did what he asked. It was like I was in shock; I literally didn't have control. Totally odd. Dave got quiet and said in a low whisper, "Lord, please come into my life." I didn't do anything. "Go ahead," Dave said very confidently.

I took a big breath, and with the sincerity of a piece of wood I said, "Lord ... please come into my life." I said it very quickly.

Like a shot of nitro, something went up my spine. I straightened up and my eyes flew open. I was staring at the ceiling when a warm flush came over me. I was shocked! I was like, "What is going on? Get me out of here!"

Dave had this grin on his face. He knew. He knew my life had just changed forever. Dave went for broke. He had been watching me in school, around town. He saw a life without Christ. He saw the inevitable destruction I would pour into my life as my sin ran unchecked. He had something for me, and I needed something from him. His message was going to offend me, no doubt.

In the weeks leading up to his getting in my face, he planned things to say, prayed for the wisdom, and went for it. Complete abandon to a cause, unwavering zealous action, unflinching, unrelenting, he offended every one of my sinful senses in the name of Christ. He took my life and ripped it up in the name of truth. He was open to my saying, "Forget you," and walking. He was willing for me to react violently. He was willing for me to talk bad about him. He was willing for me to go right back to my life and die if the message didn't hit.

Looking back, I am amazed. He brought me to the cross regardless of whether he hurt my feelings or offended me. He cared too much about my eternity and the quality of my life.

Thanks for offending me, Dave.

How many Daves are out there right now? Maybe you're a Dave. Maybe you know a Dave serving in some foreign country, facing all kinds of crazy situations. How many of us are being Dave in our neighborhoods, communities, and churches? Was my changed life worth Dave's time?

The church needs a good kick in the pants. We need to stop talking, meeting, deciding what's next, and get on with the business of evangelizing. This country is the Holy Grail when it comes to evangelizing. We have the big fat First Amendment staring us in the face. The First Amendment guarantees us the right to offend in the name of Christ. So ... who do you want to offend?

TITUS 3:1-11 *Remind the people to be subject to rulers and authorities, to be obedient, to be ready to do whatever is good, to slander no one, to be peaceable and considerate, and to show true humility toward all men.*

At one time we too were foolish, disobedient, deceived and enslaved by all kinds of passions and pleasures. We lived in malice and envy, being hated and hating one another. But when the kindness and love of God our Savior appeared, he saved us, not because of righteous things we had done, but because of his mercy. He saved us through the washing of rebirth and renewal by the Holy Spirit, whom he poured out on us generously through Jesus Christ our Savior, so that,

*having been justified by his grace, we might become
heirs having the hope of eternal life. This is a trustworthy saying. And I want you to stress these things, so
that those who have trusted in God may be careful to
devote themselves to doing what is good. These
things are excellent and profitable for everyone.*

*But avoid foolish controversies and genealogies and
arguments and quarrels about the law, because these
are unprofitable and useless. Warn a divisive person
once, and then warn him a second time. After that, have
nothing to do with him. You may be sure that such a
man is warped and sinful; he is self-condemned.*

My prideful sin on any given day can lead me into areas of offense. Lately I have been struggling with "Super Christians."
These are Christians who love the inner debate among
Christians; the Christian cops, if you will. They add nothing to
the landscape of faith other than self-induced bloviating
about why they are right and you are wrong. The Super Christians do a great job of throwing the Word of God in your face,
all the while baiting you into public debate. Using worldly offense as their weapon, Super Christians serve no purpose
other than dividing Christian against Christian.

3.4
MAKE 'EM
REALLY MAD

Now I understand that last paragraph is harsh, but this is
what I'm thinking. I have a hard time loving these people.
When I engage them, I want to rip their faces off. I am not
proud of this, and I'm not sharing this to prop myself up. I'm
just saying this is a big source of worldly sinful offense for
me.

I had the dubious responsibility of answering the e-mail at
X3church, where I wound up hearing from a lot of Super
Christians. Eventually, I couldn't handle it anymore, so I
passed the responsibility on to J.R. ...

And it's a responsibility I take very seriously. As you can
imagine, we get our share of crazy e-mails, and for the most
part, we ignore them. But the Super Christians love to bait
us into less-than-worthwhile communication, and sometimes

the e-mails bother me so much, I cuss at the screen while forming my reply.

One morning I was minding my own business and *bing!* an e-mail pops in with the subject line "I like what you're doing, but …" Right off the bat, I go into Defend Mode, which, if left unchecked, eventually turns into Offend Mode and ultimately causes hurt.

Here's the e-mail:

How come I can't find a clear presentation of the gospel anywhere on your site?

I guess that question has to be answered first before I decide anything about xxxchurch. You talk a bit about Jesus, but after seeing your site, I'm left with no idea of how to "get Jesus," or how He is the key to ridding me of porn. Just a warm fuzzy.

I really want your ministry to work. It's important, but your theology isn't at all clear.

Charlie

Hopefully, this will be taken as coaching and not stone throwing.

The truth about Charlie's e-mail is that I agree with a few things he has to say. I agree ministries need a clear presentation of the gospel. I agree Jesus should be accessible to the general public should they need questions answered. But, and there is always a but, I got offended. Not the offense caused by Christ in love and truth, but the kind of offense that makes me want to rip this guy's head off. That's the truth. He pressed my buttons and I lost it, because I reacted to his actions and not his heart. The e-mail made me mad. Perhaps it makes you mad. Perhaps you can't see the problem. Perhaps I need anger management.

I wasted no time hitting the reply button, but for the next

several minutes I did waste my time—and Charlie's—going for broke. I crafted an e-mail that would nail him, make him feel stupid. I wanted this guy to think about every e-mail he sent for the rest of his life.

Sin, sin, sin. Plain and simple. I left the comfort of Christ and fell right back on my sinful desires of pride. This was going through my mind as I was writing: *How dare this guy! Who does he think he is! Doesn't he know who I am? Doesn't he know how many people we help?* My prideful sin bore itself out in offense. The truth about this is hard for me to take. It means I have some growing up to do. I have to change. It means I have a lot to pray about, a lot to confess and a lot to stay accountable for, and I must ask forgiveness. This is *not* offending like Jesus.

Here was my response to Charlie.

Charlie,

Yeah, I see your point ... talking a little bit about Jesus just doesn't cut it.... Thanks. We're gonna shut the whole thing down and when we come back we're gonna do nothing but scream the gospel from the top of our lungs 24/7 without stopping, ever ... just like you do in your everyday life ... I mean, you do talk about him 24/7 without having any other conversations, right? I would hate to think you talk about other things to people as you get to know them ... I mean, I don't know how I could like you if you don't talk about Jesus 24/7 all the time without ceasing, not stopping and never ending ... please tell me you do, please. I want to like you....

Thanks,
J.R.
X3church

While I was writing, it seemed so great, so right. After the fact? Not so great. I had been proud of my response.

Look how crafty I am; look at the point I managed to prove.

It was only a few hours later that day when I began to hear the Holy Spirit whisper softly yet steadily, *Are you sure you should have done that? Did you do the right thing?* The questions kept coming the rest of the day. I did my best to run away from the truth. I beat this guy up the rest of the day. I told my wife about him, calling Charlie an idiot.

By the time I hit my knees that night, the Holy Spirit was up in my grill. I could not hide; I confessed my sin right then and there. I was ashamed and guilty. There I was, on my knees, alone like so many times before, asking forgiveness for my actions. I looked up at God and thought, *Will I ever not do things like this? Will I ever be able to contain my pride and not react or retaliate when I'm offended?*

Regardless of where Charlie and I disagree or agree, I didn't need to strike out. I am a man in need of Christ more and more every day. I am easily offended and easily given to prideful anger. These are things I must cut out of my life through constant attention, through prayer, and through personal accountability. Charlie did his job offending like Christ in my life. I should have carefully read through his words to see his concern. Instead, I did everything I could to be like a Super Christian.

To date I have not asked forgiveness from Charlie. I justify it. I say to myself, *The guy's a jerk, Super Christian. I am not going to waste my time.* The truth? I must ask forgiveness.

Ultimately, my reply e-mail found a national audience. It seems Charlie got offended too. He called a national Christian radio talk show a few days after my e-mail came back to him. The host of the show, a very recognizable Christian personality, was happy to talk about the infraction. He read both e-mails on the air and took some phone calls about the offense. The segment prompted dozens of e-mails back to XXXchurch.com, all asking the same question: "What were you thinking?" I wasn't. That day two Scriptures pounded in my head.

An offended brother is more unyielding than a fortified city, and disputes are like the barred gates of a citadel.

PROVERBS 18:19

And …

But since he has no root, he lasts only a short time. When trouble or persecution comes because of the word, he quickly falls away.

MATTHEW 13:21

My offense created hurt, hypocrisy, and division. My sin hit the rooftops. Neither Charlie, nor the ministry, nor I fared well. The wages of sin is death and sometimes that death comes in the form of strained and tattered relationships, Christian to Christian. Charlie, if you're reading this … I'm sorry for offending you. Sorry, Charlie.

Dear friends, do not believe every spirit, but test the spirits to see whether they are from God, because many false prophets have gone out into the world. This is how you can recognize the Spirit of God: Every spirit that acknowledges that Jesus Christ has come in the flesh is from God, but every spirit that does not acknowledge Jesus is not from God. This is the spirit of the antichrist, which you have heard is coming and even now is already in the world.

You, dear children, are from God and have overcome them, because the one who is in you is greater than the one who is in the world. They are from the world and therefore speak from the viewpoint of the world, and the world listens to them. We are from God, and whoever knows God listens to us; but whoever is not from God does not listen to us. This is how we recognize the Spirit of truth and the spirit of falsehood.

1 JOHN 4:1-6

There's a saying in Alcoholics Anonymous: "Every new meeting starts with resentment and a coffeepot." It speaks so clearly to the nature of offenses. I'm fairly certain AA stole it from the church.

3.5 OFFEND FOR CHRIST

We have more Christian denominations than Target has stuff for sale under a hundred bucks. The church of Jesus Christ seems to be the dollar store of faith, where, if you just keep looking, sooner or later you'll find what you want. Each denomination would like to think it is the only one dressed to speak about truth, discernment, and evangelizing. We love putting everyone's ministry under the microscope and deciding which one is good, which one is bad.

When J.R. and I roll out a new outreach, we keep one thing in mind: "Anything goes, short of sin." Push the envelope. Walk on the edge. Offend like Jesus. When you offend like Jesus, you're willing to scratch the surface of sin in people's lives. You are willing to get involved with people. One-on-one, face-to-face. You will want people to answer one very important question: "Who is Christ?"

Simon Peter faced this question from Jesus.

MATTHEW 16:13-20

When Jesus came to the region of Caesarea Philippi, he asked his disciples, "Who do people say the Son of Man is?"

They replied, "Some say John the Baptist; others say Elijah; and still others, Jeremiah or one of the prophets."

"But what about you?" he asked. "Who do you say I am?"

Simon Peter answered, "You are the Christ, the Son of the living God."

Jesus replied, "Blessed are you, Simon son of Jonah, for this was not revealed to you by man, but by my Father in heaven. And I tell you that you are Peter, and on this rock I will build my church, and the gates of Hades will not overcome it. I will give you the keys of the kingdom of heaven; whatever you bind on earth will be bound in heaven, and whatever you loose on earth will be loosed in heaven." Then he warned his disciples not to tell anyone that he was the Christ.

Simon answered, and Jesus said something that changed the way I tell people about Christ. He said, "This was not revealed to you by man, but by my Father in heaven." We must be in a position to ask the question and let God the Father reveal the answer. I can't tell you how many times I would be faced with someone answering this question, and I would sell, trade, make a deal, put a bow on it—all in the name of a conversion. Why let God get involved? I was doing a fine job without him.

Whether it's porn-show outreach, feeding the homeless, or painting your neighbor's house, we must meet people the same way Jesus did—unafraid of what the truth will do for them.

Since Christ first asked, "Who do you say I am?" we have been chasing our tails to come up with the causes and conditions for asking the question. Collectively, we love giving altar calls, handing out tracts, holding tent revivals, buying millions of dollars of TV time, hiring marketing professionals, and building giant buildings. There is no wrong way to reach out if you settle on Christ as Savior.

You will take heat if you start asking the question. Get accountability for everything you do concerning outreach. Set yourself up to succeed. Take on outreach that suits your personality, your lifestyle, your way of thinking. Take on outreach directly around you. Whatever that means. Just get the conversation started about Christ.

Though I am free and belong to no man, I make myself a slave to everyone, to win as many as possible. To the Jews I became like a Jew, to win the Jews. To those under the law I became like one under the law (though I myself am not under the law), so as to win those under the law. To those not having the law I became like one not having the law (though I am not free from God's law but am under Christ's law), so as to win those not having the law. To the weak I became weak, to win the weak. I have become all things to all men so that by all possible means I might save some. I do all this for the sake of the gospel that I may share in its blessings.

1 CORINTHIANS 9:19-23

Christianity sits on the hottest social issues in the world, and they're all contained within the pages of the Bible. Should you need to know which way to go on an issue, crack it open. Causes need excitement, and excitement causes the world to notice and get involved. Involvement doesn't necessarily equal participation; involvement could mean opposition, but even the latter will get people talking.

People ask us all the time, "What can I do to help?" We say very directly, "What do you believe in? What do you *want* to tell the world? What do you *need* to tell the world? What does God want to tell the world?"

Perhaps more than anyone in history, Paul understood his role of offending like Jesus. We often like to dismiss Scriptures from Paul, because they make us responsible to all the people around us. Paul says, "By all possible means I might save some" (1 Cor. 9:22). All possible means. That Scripture is not a loaded gun giving you license to be a complete idiot in the name of Christ, but it is the freedom to go, do, and say what you need to. To say it to anyone, anywhere, at any time. Actually, it is a responsibility.

When you do decide to offend like Jesus, you will often think you're wrong. You will want to quit. You will wonder if you're doing any good. Let all the doubts and uncertainty be your benchmark for success, because I guarantee you: If you doubt yourself and your work, you are on the right track.

Be outrageous. Challenge everyone around you, whether they are in faith or not. Use wild and way-out tactics. Whatever rules you are presently under in your faith or denomination? Break them. Be bold for Christ. Be creative for him. Shake it up and mix it up. Offend like Jesus.

CHAPTER
RAGING DIVINITY

CH 4 | RAGING DIVINITY

Jesus went through all the towns and villages, teaching in their synagogues, preaching the good news of the kingdom and healing every disease and sickness. When he saw the crowds, he had compassion on them, because they were harassed and helpless, like sheep without a shepherd. Then he said to his disciples, "The harvest is plentiful but the workers are few. Ask the Lord of the harvest, therefore, to send out workers into his harvest field."

MATTHEW
9:35-38

Since I was a kid, it's been one question after the other: What are you going to be? Where are you going to school? Are you going to get married? Are you going to stop drinking? Why do you cuss so much? Do you know who Christ is? What's your calling?

4.1
THE CALL

What's my *calling?* Who said anything about a calling? When did I miss the class about callings? Aren't callings for Catholic priests or something?

After I got saved, it seemed of paramount importance in my little circle of saved people to have a calling. All around me, they were dropping like flies as the newly saved folks were getting their callings. It was like waiting for your college acceptance letter. Some were saying things like "God wants me to do this," "God wants me to do that," and I was like, "What are you talking about?" The last time I'd talked to God, he was kicking the crap out of me in some kitchen in Cleveland.

Conversations about callings should always start, "Where were you before your call?" or "Where do you feel you are being called right now?" The answers should be well thought out as you wrap yourself around the idea that God calls you to Christ. That's it. He calls you away from sin and calls you to serve. It's the latter that somehow always finds the cutting-room floor.

4.2
BC: BEFORE
THE CALL

The twelve disciples were minding their own business and *bam!* there's Jesus smiling, saying, "Come, follow me." Off they went. Can you imagine? They went!

Today you can't go to church without the signs smacking you in the face: "Leadership Training Class," "Be a Great Leader Seminar." From the looks of it, you'd think we just don't have enough leaders. The modern-day church loves its conferences, seminars, and training methods. With titles such as "Life Cycle of a Leader" and "Forty Days of Purpose," it's easy to understand why we flock to classrooms and churches all over the country to try to understand our fate. We all want purpose; we all want that magic bullet that will put us on solid ground with God. I do. The thing about your calling is it's actually quite easy to understand.

Can you name the most common item in any church's lost and found? Give up? It's the Bible. Go figure. Other than its being one of the dustiest books on many shelves and nightstands, the Bible holds the very magic bullet we seek. Hard to believe, I know, but it's true. Anytime, anywhere, there's more calling going on in the Bible than to your average Christian TV show's 800 number.

Of course, there is a calling on your life. You would hardly be a Christian if you didn't have a call. God makes certain demands of us as we come to him, but one demand that always seems to get buried in those leadership seminars comes in the form of a parable. In Luke 14, Jesus talks about a great banquet and how great it will be, but how we must call people to the table.

LUKE 14:23   *Then the master told his servant, "Go out to the*
roads and country lanes and make them come in, so
that my house will be full."

What's great about Luke 14:23? It's followed up with Jesus talking about the cost of being a disciple. Not a leader, but a disciple. So within a couple of chapters you get a great big call on your life: "Go get some people for the cool banquet," and then Jesus tells you what that will look like as you do it. It's so simple, so easy to understand, it's hard to believe. No conference needed. Easy like Sunday morning. So if you read Luke 14 and draw it into your life, Jesus is calling you to evangelize.

The truth, albeit hard to take, about church people is we generally do not want to get out of the pews. We have worked ourselves into comfortable lifestyles that rarely encompass others and their needs.

4.3
WHAT'S
REALLY GOING
ON?

J.R. and I were in Michigan one weekend doing a porn talk for a small church outside of Grand Rapids. We loved the people and the way they presented themselves to the community. Not that it matters, but we were highly impressed. We see a lot of churches throughout the year, and this one was right on track. The leaders greeted us with smiles and made our stay nothing short of spectacular. We didn't want to leave on Sunday.

That weekend in Michigan, we found ourselves wanting to hang with the leaders of that small church. We would have lived with those guys; they were simply great people with big hearts, concerned about the people in the church and the community they served. Sometimes as we travel, we get a really good look at modern-day disciples; that weekend, we got a great look.

On Sunday morning as the lead pastor introduced me, he said something to the congregation that really smacked me: "You have entrusted me and the leaders of this church to lead you and your families. Today we have a message we feel needs to be heard." His words, sincere and humble. He wanted to help whoever he could, any way he could.

What hit me was the pastor's sincerity in serving his church. I have heard other pastors say the exact same thing—even I have uttered those same words, but this guy hit the button that made me see the importance of having a strong, humble leader, a strong shepherd: a guy who understands that his struggles are others' struggles;

a guy who flushes out social issues and complex subjects in the name of Christ, so his sheep can go about their lives as comfortably as possible; a guy who sees himself as a disciple, not a leader.

2 PETER 1:3-11   *His divine power has given us everything we need for life and godliness through our knowledge of him who called us by his own glory and goodness. Through these he has given us his very great and precious promises, so that through them you may participate in the divine nature and escape the corruption in the world caused by evil desires.*

For this very reason, make every effort to add to your faith goodness; and to goodness, knowledge; and to knowledge, self-control; and to self-control, perseverance; and to perseverance, godliness; and to godliness, brotherly kindness; and to brotherly kindness, love. For if you possess these qualities in increasing measure, they will keep you from being ineffective and unproductive in your knowledge of our Lord Jesus Christ. But if anyone does not have them, he is nearsighted and blind, and has forgotten that he has been cleansed from his past sins.

Therefore, my brothers, be all the more eager to make your calling and election sure. For if you do these things, you will never fall, and you will receive a rich welcome into the eternal kingdom of our Lord and Savior Jesus Christ.

4.4
NEVER FALL

My favorite line in this passage is verse 10: "Therefore, my brothers, be all the more eager to make your calling and election sure. For if you do these things, you will never fall." Sometimes I feel as if I'm the only guy who has ever read that line. Never fall. For a guy like me, that's big, considering I spent the majority of my life before Christ falling and not caring about getting up. Then I met Christ and *boom!* At times it seems too much, until I get to that verse and God throws out a big fat promise: "if." And there is always an if. If I take some responsibility for myself. The responsibility comes in verses 5–7.

When I was saved in 1985, I needed huge amounts of discipline in my life. God led me to a guy named Tommy Cusaic. Tommy was a dockworker in Cleveland, Ohio—a gruff, tough old dude. His fingers looked like mini-sledgehammers, his hair was white as snow, and his voice was like a fading foghorn. He was to become my worst nightmare and my guidepost for what a disciple looked like.

Tommy did everything he could to help me see my worth in the Lord, something that was lost on me for a while. He had a thundering velvet hand; he was quick to praise and quick to correct. We would spend hours talking about what it meant to be a Christian and what it meant to be a man of God.

Tommy brought me to life as he pushed me closer to God through prayer and studying the Bible. He used words like *sacrifice, generosity, selflessness,* and *love.* He asked me if I had something to give to the world. He challenged me to get up and do something for others, instead of always worrying about myself. On occasion, he would jam his finger in my chest and remind me I am to be a servant, not a punk.

He was a master at helping people understand who they were and what that meant to Christ. Tommy helped me define who I was and the behavior God called me away from; he helped me shake off the doubts and uncertainty about my newfound faith. He was a concrete example of a man living in obedience to God.

He was a disciple, living out his calling.

Tommy was an unsuspecting leader in the body of Christ. He wasn't a pastor, elder, board member, usher. He never took a class or attended a seminar. He was a ground trooper who read the Word and put its practicality to work in his life. He was an ordinary dockworker capable of leading people to Christ. He exhibited a living example of discipleship and helped me understand that my calling was all sewn up in the Word of God and that if I had to guess at what God was doing with my life, either I was not listening, or I was lying to myself.

4.5
WHAT DOES IT
LOOK LIKE?

We are filled to the rafters with courses, classes, and books about what church leaders should look like. Everything from the cool guy in the youth group to the dude on TV asking for ten bucks. Today's Christian leaders sound more like Tony Robbins than Tony Robbins himself. We have dressed up the word *leader* in a crazy suit and sent it off to street corners around the world, screaming, "God hates everything, and you're going to hell!"

Collectively, our Christian mainstream leadership has stopped saying anything about anything. Today's leaders are so caught up in not pissing anyone off that they smile at sin and look the other way, hoping God will deal with it. We do not lead, we placate. We have forgotten what it's like to express the truth among those we serve. Sheep need a shepherd, not a leader.

The body of Christ has become obsessed with leadership to the point of exhaustion. A very unscientific Google search for the words *church* and *leaders* produced 70,300,000 hits. Another unscientific Google search for the word *disciples* produced 27,300,000 hits. Google is slowly becoming the world's new Bible.

JOHN 15:18-25

If the world hates you, keep in mind that it hated me first. If you belonged to the world, it would love you as its own. As it is, you do not belong to the world, but I have chosen you out of the world. That is why the world hates you. Remember the words I spoke to you: "No servant is greater than his master." If they persecuted me, they will persecute you also. If they obeyed my teaching, they will obey yours also. They will treat you this way because of my name, for they do not know the One who sent me. If I had not

*come and spoken to them, they would not be guilty
of sin. Now, however, they have no excuse for their
sin. He who hates me hates my Father as well. If I
had not done among them what no one else did,
they would not be guilty of sin. But now they have
seen these miracles, and yet they have hated both
me and my Father. But this is to fulfill what is written in their Law: "They hated me without reason."*

For the longest time I would not call myself a disciple. The very word made me flinch. I bought all the garbage the church and the world had heaped on this word. I didn't want to be a freak. I didn't want bumper stickers on my car. I didn't want to upset my life for Christ. People would ask if I was a Christian, and I would sheepishly say yes. A Christian? Yes. A disciple? No! That would mean I was a little off or weird. It meant dying and following.

4.6
J.R.'S LIST

I had it all worked out, and I was not going to be a disciple. My fear was that I would lose myself in the mix. For the most part, I liked what I saw in the mirror, and I didn't want to go over the edge. Being a full-fledged disciple meant robes, protest signs, and poverty, right?

I was highly deceived.

God was banging on me about this for what seemed like years. He was asking, *What is so wrong with me that you can't be a part of the club?* I had no answer. I was scared I would turn into one of those pastors and church leaders I saw on Sunday. I wanted nothing to do with those guys. They were the very people I had been running from my entire life.

Me, be a disciple? No way!

One morning I was praying and just being quiet with God, and he came calling. *What is a disciple?* he asked. I had no answer for him, nothing, nada. I was embarrassed. At the time I was the guy at the Bible study who offered up all the right answers and got people to take sides on issues. I was the guy leading the charge to read the Word, and I couldn't answer one simple question. What an idiot I was. God asked one simple question, and I couldn't even give him a made-up answer. All day long, the question ran through my mind, and all day long I had nothing. God was in my grill every hour of that day pushing me to the Word. *J.R.!* he was saying. *Come to me.*

I got home that night exhausted from the torment going on in my head. I grabbed my Bible and sat on the bed. I hit Matthew, Mark, Luke, John, and it smacked me in the face: The disciples were the biggest bunch of regular, run-of-the-mill, faithless guys the world had ever known ... just like me. They doubted, they stumbled, they denied ... they were essentially idiots like me. I could hear God laughing as he watched me come closer to him.

That night I cried as I prayed, not a light little cry, but that crazy, can't-catch-your-breath crying, the kind that makes noise like the sound of a jet taking off. I was so grateful for the Word of God. For the first time in my life, I had purpose; for the first time in my life I had a title: disciple.

The next day, I made a list, a reminder of sorts. I needed to keep myself honest with the Lord and the world around me. My pride and ego often crush those around me. In an instant, I can bring pain and sorrow to my life and the lives of others. This list still serves as a guide for all that I am and all that I need to be:

A disciple doubts.
A disciple deceives.
A disciple denies.
A disciple forgets.
A disciple fears.
A disciple changes lives.
A disciple is arrogant.
A disciple denies himself.
A disciple believes Jesus is Savior.
A disciple heals.

A disciple leads.

A disciple hides.

A disciple is human.

A disciple loves.

A disciple protects.

A disciple is radical.

A disciple is lost.

A disciple is healed.

A disciple leaves his life.

A disciple cuts off ears.

A disciple follows Christ.

A disciple gives his life for others.

A disciple dies for faith.

A disciple sins.

A disciple is called to be a disciple.

A disciple falls away from Christ.

A disciple prays.

A disciple leads people to Christ.

A disciple gets in the grill of others.

A disciple has little faith.

A disciple has no attachment to men.

A disciple has no attachment to religion.

A disciple will write.

A disciple will teach.

A disciple will lie.

A disciple will tell the truth.

A disciple forgives.

A disciple asks for forgiveness.

A disciple rants.

A disciple travels.

A disciple fasts.

A disciple questions.

A disciple hopes.

A disciple gets angry.

A disciple does not worry.

A disciple worries.

A disciple likes money.

A disciple doesn't worry about money.

A disciple has friends.

A disciple has a church.

A disciple gives up.

My hope every day is to add and take away from this list. Today? They all fit. Tomorrow? God only knows. I'm not so interested in being a great leader. I am very interested in being a great disciple.

We need to be careful with leadership in the body of Christ. We should be slow to prop up leadership and quick to identify those committed to a life of service to God and his people. How do we spot these people? Disciples leave their lives and follow Christ. You will know them by their fruit, not their seminar-teaching experience or church-class certificates. You will not find them sitting in pews. You will find them among the wolves.

JOHN 14:12   *I tell you the truth, anyone who has faith in me will do what I have been doing. He will do even greater things than these, because I am going to the Father.*

4.7   The Word of God is no happy accident. It is quite inten-
THE TUCK   tional and definitive. If we are looking to act out faith with our calling, then the place to be is the Word of God. I am amazed at how we put our little spin on every word, verse, and chapter to suit our justification, arguments, and book agendas.

God is always retelling his story through the Word. Some call it the living Word because of this. Relationally, I am always astonished, because whatever is happening around me, the Bible seems to pick up on it and speak directly to me. God is telling you either someone else's story or your own. He walks you through the Word, clearly defining your life against the people who came before you. His Word is the truth; your problem is also the truth. So God lays down living examples readily available to anyone at any time. It's plausible, arguable, and sustainable. It is you: who you were, who you are, and who you will be.

God likes to do "The Tuck" in the Word. The Tuck is that one word, one story, one eye-opening chapter that you have read a hundred times before it beats you over the head and *wham!* a little truth leaks into your life. That's The Tuck.

The great thing about The Tuck is that God usually lets it go when you are ignoring him. We are always blaming God for not being communicative; the truth is, we are the usual suspects in this scenario. We stop the flow of information between the Father and us. He is constantly asking us questions about our lives through the Holy Spirit. He is always calling, but we rarely pick up. The apostle John says, "In the beginning was the Word, and the Word was with God, and the Word was God" (John 1:1). The Word was God. The Tuck helps us stay alive in the Word.

I needed The Tuck about a year ago. I was consumed with doing something new and out-front for the Lord. I hit the Word headfirst, looking and looking and looking for that one pearl I knew God had for me. I exhausted myself. I got physically tired from looking. I began to think God didn't have anything for me, and I got bummed. In disbelief, I thought, *How could he have nothing for me?*

I gave up on a Saturday. Since I am so prone to wander, I nonchalantly said to myself, *If he needs me, he'll let me know.* But this "disciple" doubted God had anything for me, and my first reaction to not having my needs met was "I'm out."

The next day (Sunday) I was sitting in my stew, and I heard God calling me as I stared at my Bible on the couch. I reluctantly grabbed it and flipped through the New Testament, less than sure I'd see anything. I came to Romans and found myself staring at chapter 16. Perhaps you know this one already. It's Paul's greetings, the part of Romans we always tend to skip: Paul saying hello to everyone and their mother.

So here I am, distant with God because I'm a jerk, and he pulls out a Tuck so massive in my life, it led me to a new friend and the creation of this book. Some say Tertius was a secretary, a scribe, a friend. The apostle Paul knew him as a professional. Paul understood the powerful task of moving the truth to an audience. Paul understood the training, the experience, the language skills, and the knowledge of the law it took to be a great scribe, a great communicator. Tertius says hello to the world in Romans 16:22. I have read Romans a handful of times, and every time I glossed over Tertius and his howdy-do as insignificant along the sovereign time line of God.

And then it hit me: Tertius wrote Romans! Read it. If we rely on history, Tertius is a hand that held a pen, nothing more. The only problem? God saw fit to mention him by name in the context of one of the most powerful books in the New Testament. To excuse this divine act is to ignore Tertius's talent, which brought the book of Romans to life for you and me.

The scribes of Paul's time were the keepers, disseminators, and publishers of information. They researched, wrote, and pushed it out to the world. It is God who gave the world its first look at a disciple who could communicate the gospel to a mass audience. History would suggest that Tertius was paid by the word. The book of Romans has more than seventy-five hundred words. Paul got his money's worth, and we are reaping the benefits of that invoice two thousand years later.

It is inconceivable to think God would have handed over such a task to just a hand and a pen. God understood the need for his words to be crafted in such ways as to withstand the test of time. He understood the writing talent needed to communicate a large message. He knew not just any dude would do. Perhaps Tertius gets to say hello because we need to know how God used his talents to deliver the message of Christ to the world. Perhaps God needs you to do the same thing with your talent, no matter how bland or obscure you think it is.

There I was, visibly shaken (I'm a Bible geek that way), sitting on the couch with this new understanding. Paul needed help. Better yet, he asked for help. Paul—the guy who wrote most of the New Testament—asked for help! I guess I always put these dudes so high up in the air that I think angels and spiritual stuff were always surrounding them. Turns out everyone needs a little help. God gave Paul help in the form of Tertius, not another apostle or some high-and-mighty Bible guy. No, he was a scribe, a run-of-the-mill scribe who probably had no idea what he was getting into.

At the time I realized this, I was struggling with my own creative endeavors for the Lord. I was reaching out to God, asking him to point me in the right direction so I, too, could impact the kingdom for Christ. I am a regular guy with a modicum of talent and a whole lot of apprehension about what to say and who to say it to. I would imagine Tertius felt the same way. Tertius's howdy-do was no accident; it's real, and God tucked it in there so you and I could understand. The face of a disciple doesn't always need a spotlight or a locked-down audience; it only needs to be of service. In this case, it only needed a pen.

My prayer is not that you take them out of the world but that you protect them from the evil one. They are not of the world, even as I am not of it. Sanctify them by the truth; your word is truth. As you sent me into the world, I have sent them into the world. For them I sanctify myself, that they too may be truly sanctified.

JOHN 17:15-19

The church often struggles with this prayer. While we have diverse opinions about the world and our place in it, we must understand that Jesus prayed that prayer in John 17 because he was preparing to leave the earth. He was imploring the

4.8
GETTING
THERE

Father to take care of his disciples. Christ knew the job of disciples; he knew they would face the Evil One, so he asked God, "Please take care of them." Can you imagine being Jesus, hanging out with these ragtag guys and still seeing past them with the understanding they would build the world a church? I sometimes think about what the world would have been like without that prayer, and I thank Jesus for praying it.

He also prayed it in front of them so they could hear his concerns. Have you ever done that? In the ministry, we call those "backdoor prayers." It's the passive-aggressive form of prayer. Imagine you are one of the original disciples and you just heard Jesus lay down the plan. Then he starts praying to lock the deal. I would have said, "Time out, Lord! You mean to tell me you're leaving, and there's a good chance I am going to face evil as I go into the world for you? I don't think so." That was a tall order for anyone. That prayer locked it down for the disciples, giving them the game plan for the biggest job the world has ever known.

The definitive plan about where and when is found in that prayer. The "where" is the space you find at the end of your arms. I know some of us are all geeked up to go to Africa, China, or Iraq for foreign missions—it's all good—just make sure your efforts are for the glory of God and not some vicarious high from an Indiana Jones movie.

The "when" of that prayer is now. Look up from this book, and think about that one person you know who could use the love of a Savior.... Now go. Put the book down—you won't hurt our feelings—and let that person know what Jesus has done for you. Tell him or her about those moments when you are alone with God and you just smile to yourself, because he is alive in you. Tell the person you don't want or need anymore. Tell them you don't search anymore. Tell them how the trappings of the world don't excite you anymore. Tell that person their Savior loved them so much, he prayed for them two thousand years ago.

Again, easy like Sunday morning. The call, the action, within one page. Christ was so inclined, he even prayed for those we would talk to as we went into the world.

My prayer is not for them alone. I pray also for those   JOHN 17:20-26
who will believe in me through their message, that
all of them may be one, Father, just as you are in me
and I am in you. May they also be in us so that the
world may believe that you have sent me. I have
given them the glory that you gave me, that they
may be one as we are one: I in them and you in me.
May they be brought to complete unity to let the
world know that you sent me and have loved them
even as you have loved me.

Father, I want those you have given me to be with
me where I am, and to see my glory, the glory you
have given me because you loved me before the
creation of the world.

Righteous Father, though the world does not
know you, I know you, and they know that you have
sent me. I have made you known to them, and will
continue to make you known in order that the love
you have for me may be in them and that I myself
may be in them.

Jesus understood the world would need us. He knew the world would be looking for us. We have to bust out of the exclusive nature we have built around Christianity. Let go of all the Super-Christian garbage and run into the world as fast as we can, knowing Christ himself went to the Father on our behalf, asking him to protect us. He will. It's okay to bring the message of Christ into the world. It really is. That's his call.

Show up.

Simon answered, "Master, we've worked hard all   LUKE 5:5
night and haven't caught anything. But because you
say so, I will let down the nets."

4.9
SHOW UP

Callings have a way of sneaking up on you. One day you're a power-wielding TV producer yelling at people for not putting enough smut on the tube, the next day you're flat on your face, hoping when you look up you don't see Christ smiling back at you.

There's a great deal of discussion about "calling"—the kind of discussion that always seems to end with no definitive plan and a whole lot of speculation. If we told you it's all right not to be a leader or to have a definitive look at your future, would you feel any better about your "Christian position"?

Both J.R. and I struggled for years with the issues of leadership and discipleship. For the longest time, we were thinking we missed the leadership boat. Discipleship was a reserved position for those much more spiritual than us. We didn't understand that Jesus really just wants us to show up.

4.10
ONE
QUESTION, J.R.

The other day I had a conversation with a kid I mentor. Mark is his name; he's a good kid. He had some problems with drugs and his parents. Now he finds himself in front of Christ, wondering what's next. We were going to a movie, and he was quiet on the ride over, so I chased him up a tree and made him talk about what's going on.

"J.R.," he said, "is it all right to start a Bible study and not tell anyone at the church?"

Honestly, I expected him to tell me he was smoking pot or having sex or something. I was relieved, yet dumbfounded as to where he got the idea that he needed permission to talk about the Word of God.

"Let me tell you something, Mark," I said in a low and strong voice, trying to be a good leader and mentor. "You do whatever you need to do. If you're talking about God and trying to help build others in Christ, you never need permission to do anything, only good counsel. What the church is missing are guys like you willing to get something going."

"Okay," he said, like nothing just happened.

"What made you think you had to ask permission to start a Bible study?" I asked.

His answer is still ringing in my head: "I didn't want to make anybody mad." Translation: He got the message from someone inside our little church circle that there are certain clauses and conditions for talking about God.

Mark explained that he felt if he did something outside the church, then people would think he was rocking the boat.

"Rocking the boat?!" I yelled. "That's the idea!"

Not a smile on the kid's face.

"Okay," I said, "what's the big deal if you do?"

"I don't want anyone thinking I'm, like, causing division or not liking what's going on," he said. The more we talked, the clearer it became that Mark was exercising his faith, acting on his call, and struggling every step of the way. Mark wanted to go forward but doubted his course; he wanted to have an impact on the world but worried about the people in front of him. But he was gutsy enough to talk about it, which made all the difference in the world.

God was calling Mark to act out his faith in the form of a Bible study, and he was worrying about the reaction. It may sound stupid or insignificant, but Mark had struggled for weeks about whether to even talk about it. Call it what you will, but I'm sure every one of the original disciples had the same candid thoughts about what they were doing, just like Mark did. His honesty and willingness to hang himself out there was inspiring.

I slapped him on the back as we walked into the theater. "Nice job, ya Judas," I said. "Way to go dividing the church."

"Shut up, J.R." He smiled and looked away.

Isn't it great to hear it? "Hey! (insert name here), come here. This is what I need you to do, and this is how it gets done...." The critics will say it ain't that easy. Yeah? Well, tell that to the twelve dudes who put a church on every corner of the world. Yes, you will face some stuff, no doubt, but God has prepared a way for you. Just listen and study a lot.

4.11
CALLING YOUR PRAYERS, TIME, CASH, MIND, AND COMMUNITY

So ... here it is. The Starving Jesus Five. Five great ways to keep your calling hopping and your faith in action.

4.11.1
YOUR PRAYERS Keep a very active prayer life. The Bible says to "pray continually" (1 Thess. 5:17). Prayer is the one thing you can always count on. When other people fail you, when your day sucks, when you doubt, when you fear, when you just need peace—pray. Build routine into your prayer life. Jesus would find solitude and pray often. Do it in the morning and at night. If you easily forget, write a note, and stick it to your bathroom mirror. The great thing about prayer is that it's one thing you will be drawn to as you increase your study of the Bible. Every now and then while you are praying, just be quiet. Listen. I know it's a stretch to get away from the TV, the iPod, the computer, or even your family, but go, be quiet. Listen. He has a lot to say to you. Pray.

4.11.2
YOUR TIME Let's think about time in terms of two: (1) your time spent drawing closer to God and (2) your time as a blessing to other people. God is always looking to draw close to you. He made you. He wants your time. Study his words. Pray, meditate, look for him in everything you do. Give freely of your time to those around you. People are easy to find; you pass them every day. Slow down. Does your neighbor need something? Paint on the house? The yard mowed? Does that friend at work need to hear your story? What about your siblings? When was the last time you called and just laughed with them? If you are so inclined, hit a homeless shelter or jail. Or simply ask God where he needs you in your community. He will answer, if you're honestly looking. Do.

4.11.3
YOUR CASH God forbid I get in your pocket, but ... it's all God's. If you know him, then this is a no-brainer. We live in a world dominated by the dollar, and the cold hard reality is it takes cash to get things done. Find that one thing, that one cause in the name of Christ, and then give until it hurts.

"But I'm a college student."

"But I have kids."

"But I just got married."

"But I'm only a kid."

Listen, this is not something to think about only when the basket is getting jammed in your face. This is you letting God know where your heart and faith live. Think rich young ruler, Matthew 19. Cash will either make you really happy or make you unbelievably miserable. The thing to understand is you decide which way your heart goes. Give.

It's about eight inches from ear to ear, and God wants it all. Every thought, every dirty little secret, every dream. Here's the rule for your mind: crap in, crap out. Get in the habit of looking around. What are you allowing into your brain? What are you reading, listening to, watching on TV? What are you accessing on the computer? Who are you talking to, who's listening, and what is coming out of your mouth? Most important, are you sharing it all with God? If you are, most assuredly the Holy Spirit will guide your thinking and, in turn, guide your actions. Think.

4.11.4 YOUR MIND

Community is the hot word in the Christian circle these days (thank your favorite emergent for that), so far be it from us to break away from the pack. Do you break away from the pack? We suggest you don't. This might go contrary to your whole existence, but you must have community in your life. You must be a part of the body of Christ. The mouth and the butt do two completely different things, so find where you fit and hang on. It's okay to disagree with your community, it's okay to get mad at them, and it's okay to love and serve them, but please place principles above the personalities in your community. It's not okay to pack your bags and leave unless all avenues have been exhausted. We do most of the damage to Christianity ourselves. Let's limit the destruction by trying one simple thing inside our communities: Talk to one another. Share.

4.11.5 YOUR COMMUNITY

Raging Divinity says you are full of it. Full of change. Ready to take on the world with the love of Christ. In the church, it will mean many things to many people. Let's not stay exclusive as a group; let's get out of the pews and teach people outside the church. Help the world understand that the calling is salvation and not the fulfillment of a dream or career choice. Teach the world to act out in faith any way they can, short of sin.

CHAPTER
IGNORABLE CALLING
5

CH 5 | IGNORABLE CALLING

JOHN 10:1-6

"I tell you the truth, the man who does not enter the sheep pen by the gate, but climbs in by some other way, is a thief and a robber. The man who enters by the gate is the shepherd of his sheep. The watchman opens the gate for him, and the sheep listen to his voice. He calls his own sheep by name and leads them out. When he has brought out all his own, he goes on ahead of them, and his sheep follow him because they know his voice. But they will never follow a stranger; in fact, they will run away from him because they do not recognize a stranger's voice." Jesus used this figure of speech, but they did not understand what he was telling them.

Hearing from God, listening to God: However you want to put it, it's become a stop sign in the modern church. How many times do we hear the following sentence starters?

5.1
HONEST EARS

"God told me ..."

"I heard from God ..."

"God says ..."

"I think God is saying ..."

The "God told me" starter is a nonarguable point for the Born Again Lazy. That's why we use it. Kind of the nice Christian way of saying, "Get off my back!"

Recently, I listened to God. I moved my two kids and wonderful wife halfway across the country. It was a long, arduous task that took a lot out of me. The kind of experience that books are written about. It takes your present-day life and fits it squarely in a box. When you move, you get the sense that everything is very fragile.

J.R. says listening to God is easy: "Monkeys do it every day. It's just listening with an honest ear that defines your future." We are quick to put our spin on the Word of God or the prodding of the Holy Spirit. We pick and choose what we hear, where we hear it, and from whom we hear it. If it aligns with our plans, we're in. If it requires change, growth, or forgiveness, we're out. We literally decide, knowingly or unknowingly, that truth is not the refuge we seek: It's our backup plan.

Truth requires work and effort. Understanding blessing means we are willing to go to any lengths to seek the truth—a feat many don't have the stomach for.

I am not without friends when it comes to "hearing from God." I lift my head from time to time and look hard at the faces that surround me. I shake my head a lot at the stories, the scenarios, the absolutely crazy things people are doing in the name of Christ. From me to J.R. to a guy who straps horns all over his body, people are listening to God.

JOHN 1:22-23 *Finally they said, "Who are you? Give us an answer to take back to those who sent us. What do you say about yourself?"*

John replied in the words of Isaiah the prophet, "I am the voice of one calling in the desert, 'Make straight the way for the Lord.'"

5.2
HORNS

As I was packing my office for the move, I ran across a DVD from my good friend Dave. Not too long ago, Dave listened with honest ears, and now he's reaping the rewards of a life filled with obedience to God.

Dave and I met through his wife. Well, sort of. Back in high school, I took her to prom. Dave and I didn't formally meet until several years later, when he sent me an introductory e-mail. His wife, my prom date, had kept a watch on me throughout the years and told Dave what I had been up to since college. At the time, the two of them were going through their own struggles listening to God, so she thought Dave should contact me. She figured I might be a good person for him to talk to, given my crazy life.

Dave had been pursuing the Lord and music since college, and he'd landed a great job as the music director with a church in northern California. He is an amazing musician with multiple music degrees. He's a songwriter and studio musician whose work has made it to the *Billboard* charts. He's that guy at the party who plays the piano and bowls you over with talent. Dave was living the American Ministry Dream, except for that one little annoying voice prodding him to get up and get out.

For the life of him, Dave could not shake that voice.

You may know the voice. The quiet prodding that starts somewhere deep inside. It surfaces when we are alone, like a warm, sunny spring afternoon, and it cannot be ignored. We try everything known to man to escape its call, yet it gets louder every day. We become forced to make a decision about the question it asks, about its meaning.

Dave heard the voice saying things he thought he was past. He was waiting for something new, not something he thought he had a handle on. Dave had a house, wife, kids, and bills to pay. The voice seemed to be compromising all that. The voice seemed to be tearing apart his stability.

The voice didn't care a bit about Dave's plans.

Dave's e-mail came in just before noon on a Thursday. By the weekend, we were fast friends.

Craig,

I'm overwhelmed at the thought of trying to describe the journey of myself and Amy's most recent five months. I'll just try to throw the basics at you, and we can talk more about detail.

In January of this year, Amy and I went through a crazy three weeks of experiencing some ridiculously constant prodding from God to move out to Colorado Springs. We have no friends, no family, and no job that any of this is centered around. Colorado Springs is like a random spot on the map to us that we knew nothing about. As several "coincidences" came about in January, we started to take note and pray that God would simply open doors/close doors and make things as obvious as can be.

This is where the fun part of the story comes in. I love sharing this. It's the detail of all of the ways that God did open doors/close doors and make things obvious (but not so obvious as to not require a full amount of faith). We ended up taking a trip out to Colorado Springs and felt that God was continuing to nudge us in this direction. The analogy I love to share is how we came to a realization that God had given us so many signs. Ninety-nine pieces to the puzzle. And we needed to put that final piece in so we could see the picture. A piece of the puzzle called Faith. Not our plans and design on faith that would put the final piece into the picture, but a faith that said we will leave what seemed to be everything and just go. Scary, with no job and three little kids!

So at the end of this three-week period, we journaled down five pages of notes that documented how God had spoken to Amy and me.

The story only gets more exciting as stuff happened to orchestrate leaving, contacts, job, and basic new living. They happened in ways I never could have put together myself and often could only see in hindsight. These details just abundantly affirmed and confirmed our faith decision to move out.

We are still in the middle of this major transition, as I don't have any one particular job that will put food on the table. But our needs have been met, and beyond. The human side of me wants to stress and sweat about everything. What and where I will work to raise this family of five.

The men I've bumped into, the phone calls I've randomly followed up on, etc., etc., etc., have indicated to me that somewhere and somehow we will be taken care of. I've come to realize that in this process of faith, God wants us close. We get so concerned with "where is the end result!" we forget to stay close.

Every day something seems to develop and continue to show us incredible evidence that is not only comforting, but it is very tangible for me to share with both fellow Christians and non-Christians. I have had so many opportunities to do so and seen many fires ignited and seeds planted.

My passion is to figure out and enjoy what I can do strongest to serve God. Probably through unique music ministry. It may be with any one of my God-given talents or something else that I'm about to discover. I'd love to minister to guys about "guy issues," especially sexual morality. I think the fight needs to be bigger than it currently is. I'd love to continue to minister to the general public and share the gospel with them in a secularly palatable way.

So that's it. There's obviously much more. This will at least give you a piece of me.

Give me a call and we can babble through anything. I hope you find some great direction in the new stuff that seems to be cropping up for you. It sounds like we may do some stuff together. We'll see....

Peace,
Dave

Do you know a musical genius? If you do, you'll no doubt get the best part of Dave's story. In his e-mail, he mentions wanting to do what he calls "unique music ministry." Translation: Dave honks to the beat of a different honker.

A few months prior to this e-mail, Dave had organized the Christmas pageant at his church. He had gotten the idea to buy twenty bicycle horns and strap them to his body and honk out "Jingle Bells" for the finale. Can you imagine? I couldn't ... until I opened the attached video that he'd sent with his e-mail.

There was Dave, in an orange jumpsuit, with twenty horns strapped to his legs, arms, head, and chest, honking out "Jingle Bells" to a crowd of about a thousand people. He was moving his legs and arms in such a way that would make the horns honk, in time, and since Dave had altered each horn slightly so they would each have a different note, he was able to play all these recognizable melodies. It was amazing. It was the greatest thing I had ever seen. I watched it at least a hundred times that afternoon.

I called him after I watched it for the hundredth time and said, "What do you call this?" Dave very confidently replied, "I'm Dave the Horn Guy."

I didn't know what to say. On one hand, I thought he might be crazy; on the other hand, I loved it so much I wanted to be Craig the Horn Guy. Dave explained to me how God had given him this unbelievable gift of music, and it bore itself out as Dave the Horn Guy.

If you know God, you no doubt get how much sense strapping horns to your body makes. Why shouldn't a guy put on an orange suit, strap horns all over himself, and honk out songs for the Lord? Dave is probably the closest thing to a modern-day disciple this world has right now.

Dave listened to God. He left his great job and moved his kids, his wife, his entire life to Colorado Springs. God said, *Go,* and he went. God needed the Horn Guy in Colorado. Understand that this is what these scenarios look like. Dave's story is common. When you listen to Christ and follow him, it will be an adventure, filled with the outrageousness of a circus clown and the wisdom of an omniscient God.

It was a struggle for Dave at first. His wife and kids would doubt and worry about every single thing they did for weeks, but God saw them through. After all, it was God's idea. Dave wound up sharing God's gifts with the country. From appearances on *The Tonight Show with Jay Leno* to NBC's *America's Got Talent* to halftime honking performances at NBA and NHL games. He has done numerous county and state fairs around the country and is a favorite with church conferences and professional seminars everywhere. Dave even upgraded his suit with handmade bulb horns from Germany. He can play just about anything, and does.

Listening to God is not without pain, worry, or remorse. We must be bold and step out, knowing he will provide (see Matt. 6:25–34). Listening to God must become the rule for your life, not the alternative. Sinful man is geared to self-destruct, and the world cheers us on to do it. Dave the Horn Guy did one thing that will forever separate him from the pack, just like the original twelve did. Dave simply said, "Yes, I will, God."

But you, O Sovereign Lord,
  deal well with me for your name's sake;
  out of the goodness of your love, deliver me.
For I am poor and needy,
  and my heart is wounded within me.
I fade away like an evening shadow;
  I am shaken off like a locust.
My knees give way from fasting;
  my body is thin and gaunt.
I am an object of scorn to my accusers;
  when they see me, they shake their heads.

PSALM
109:21-25

I was toweling myself off after a nice, long, hot shower, feeling pretty good about myself, when I decided to do

5.3
SHHHHHHHH

The Check. You know The Check: where you stand in front of a full-length mirror and look at yourself ... naked. And I mean *really* look.

The mirror in my bathroom became a giant reality check. I chucked the towel on the floor and moved in, stopping dead as I got a full shot at my thirty-nine-year-old body. It was fat. Not obese, but about twenty pounds more than my regular weight. It looked gruesome and sent me into one of those "I suck" jags, which literally takes prayer to yank me out of.

The weight thoughts came and went throughout the day, until later that night when I was sitting on the couch, jamming chips into my pie hole at superhero speed. I was watching TBN, as I like to do, keeping up-to-date on furniture design. The preacher was talking about fasting, saying things like "Fasting is a quick way to blessing" and "You will receive many things if you fast." He even went on to say that God will bring you cash if you fast.

The chips were going in by the dozens, and I became fascinated with this guy telling me that fasting is the way to riches. Nowhere in his sermon did I hear anything about what Christ thought. I heard a lot of justification for riches through fasting; that was about it. It was enough for me to start obsessing.

I prayed that night and simply asked God, "Should I fast?" It occurred to me as I fell asleep that I could lose a whole lot of weight if I fasted. It was like a light went on: I wouldn't have to work out; I simply wouldn't eat. I had even heard on *Entertainment Tonight* that Matt Damon fasted and lost tons of weight for a film he did. This was a no-brainer: the best-laid plans of mice and Christian idiots.

The crazy thing about listening to God and acting on what he says is that if you pray and study the Bible, it increases the volume of God's voice. He simply gets louder. The more I prayed, the more recognizable fasting became. The who, why, where, and when was laid out in front of me. There was an inevitability to it. I was hearing him say, *Fast*.

What started as a rush to vanity and greed was becoming solid testimony for an ignorable calling.

My life is full of ignorables. I ignore my wife's pleas to hang up my coat. I ignore the homeless. I ignore discipline. I ignore God. When you have a relationship with Christ, he calls you to action. When heard and ignored, the resulting action will always result in failure. Always. How do you know you are ignoring God? If you're asking the question, chances are you are.

My best friend, Rob Supan, grew up in the Christian ghetto. Rob serves as a great guidepost for my crazy Christian rhetoric. At times it must seem like the ranting of a madman. Rob and I also discuss losing weight quite often. Misery loves company.

5.4
I'M IN!

I explained what had been going on during the last few weeks. Quietly I told him, "I feel like God's calling me to do a forty-day fast." It was finally out, and I heard myself say it. Why do I use those words "I feel like he is" and "I think he is"? It's not enough that he laid our lives out in the Bible, then used the Holy Spirit to bridge the discernment gap. I still have to semidoubt everything even to discuss his calling.

We are so ready to ignore, so ready to turn, so ready to wander. The alternatives to the guessing game are questions about its source. "Maybe it's the Devil" or "Maybe I'm being an idiot." We have to learn how to listen. We are caught up in the "magic" of God, not the reality of his voice in our lives. The Word will break all the argument and questioning. We must bury our doubt by studying the Bible.

Without skipping a beat, Rob said, "I'm in!"

When you fast, do not look somber as the hypocrites do, for they disfigure their faces to show men they are fasting. I tell you the truth, they have received their reward in full. But when you fast, put

MATTHEW
6:16-18

oil on your head and wash your face, so that it will
not be obvious to men that you are fasting, but only
to your Father, who is unseen; and your Father, who
sees what is done in secret, will reward you.

5.5
WHEN YOU
FAST

On January 1, 2005, Rob Supan and I listened and started a forty-day fast. No food, no nothing—just water and juice. I would love to tell you it was the greatest thing I have ever done besides marrying my wife.

I can and it was.

Any fast, regardless of its length, does one very important thing. It throws you into the presence of God. No waiting room. Immediate access to the Creator of the world. It was amazing. We were forced to deal with sin. I'm not talking about the itty-bitty issues of everyday life; I'm talking about the very things that keep you from God. Both Rob and I struggle with pride. So much so, it stops the forward progress of our lives because we are too prideful to ask for help or admit weakness.

Within the first three days, it was apparent God was going to deal with this. There was a fight going on, one that we would not win. By not eating, we exchanged our reality for God's. We became completely dependent on him, completely. I would pray, *Please help me not eat*, and he would answer by touching my life with the truth about me. If it sounds hard, it's because it is. Yet it's so quieting and so peaceful that you lose your worldly perspective for the prospect of getting closer to God.

Jesus said, "When you fast," not "if," not "maybe." He said "when." I spent eighteen years running around our little subculture professing Christ before I even fasted once. In eighteen years I heard about fasting, read about fasting, knew a few people who fasted. A few times God even called me to fast.

I ignored him—saw fasting as an ignorable calling. That was the pattern of my life: I heard it; I ignored it. Listening to God meant work, so ignoring God was the rule. I developed nice, tight justifications for why it was okay to pick and choose his will for me. I had become an expert on starving Jesus. I was willing to look at my Savior, stare him in the face, and say, "I know better than you. Now leave me alone."

I was ten days into the fast and on my knees praying, "Please, Lord, help me get through this day without food. Lord, be my strength, be my food, be everything I need today." As the words were coming out of my mouth, I felt him touch me, and he simply asked about my father: not *the* Father, but my biological father. I've not had contact with my dad for about fifteen years. No phone calls, no letters, no e-mails, nothing. Kind of like my faith. My dad and I had a falling-out that was birthed by divorce and sinful human pride. I simply told him fifteen years ago, "Stay away." It was an act of self-preservation at the time. The pain and misery of having someone in my life who was destructive drove me far away.

On your knees, listening in the midst of a fast is like having a tornado siren an inch from your ear. You will hear from God. Day ten: I'm starving, praying, and God hits me with my dad. God was calling me to forgive; he was showing me what forgiveness looked like. He was not concerned about my feelings or my dad's feelings. God wanted resolve. He needed me to understand that he forgave me for all the garbage I have brought to his table—why couldn't I do the same for my father? God turned me to Matthew 18:15 and asked if I could ignore that.

Throughout the fast, God was showing up. Rob was getting a good dose on how to be a father and husband. Rob has six kids, and with that comes a responsibility beyond my comprehension. God beat on Rob for forty days about his time and his family. Rob would start to understand God is the giver of time and that time needed respect.

On day twenty, Rob and I were on the phone talking about the halfway point when Rob said, "This thing really has nothing to do with us. This is solely about the people around us." I rolled that around in my head all afternoon.

Listening to God and acting on what God says just isn't about me. How perfectly profound.

Day forty sucked. Well, the whole last week really. Something was going on with Rob and me that we didn't expect: We were starting to mourn the end of the fast. You would think we would be excited to eat, stuff our faces with whatever. Nope. We were almost depressed at the thought of leaving this place we had found. The safety, the peace, the knowledge of self that had been gained, the insatiable appetite for prayer and study. We were bummed.

We celebrated with pizza. It was great. Our wives were mad, though. They thought pizza was too much for our systems to digest after forty days without food. Let me help everyone out: It wasn't. In fact, I can still remember what it looked like and what it felt like going down. Rob didn't utter one word during that meal; he had a constant motion going on across the table—his hands to his mouth. It was poetry in motion. Thank God for pizza.

5.6
EXIT 43

It was about thirty days after the fast, and God was still in my grill about my dad. Even after that crazy day ten, I was still ignoring God. What made matters worse, I found accountability with Rob, and he was making my life a living hell about not contacting my dad.

I sat down at the computer, did a few Google searches, and found my dad's address. My heart was beating hard. This was a guy I had sworn dead in my life. I had actually said out loud, I would never forgive this guy. I could hear God: *I taught you forgiveness. You must exercise your faith in action.* So I wrote a very simple letter:

Hi,
   It's J.R. I think it's time we had lunch.
                             J.R.

It's funny—as I wrote that letter, I felt the years rip away from me. God had shown me forgiveness in the form of his Son and my dad. I had overlooked that picture for a lot of years. I started to get excited to see him, to talk to him, to have a dad again. I was putting the letter in the mailbox, and I couldn't help but pray he would receive it with the sincerity in which it was written. I was content.

My dad called three days later, and we talked for two minutes. Two minutes! It was good, really good. We planned to meet halfway between the two of us—Exit 43 off Interstate 76.

We met, and it was good. The years left us, and so did all the garbage we brought to the table. He asked me why I wrote, and I said, "Because I finally listened to God." He smiled and said, "I have been waiting a long time for this, thank God." I can't remember what we ate, but we talked for hours. The last fifteen years condensed into sentences like "It's good to see you," "Do you like to fish?" "Let's plan a weekend, so I can meet your wife."

You'd think it would have been crazy awkward and uncomfortable, but God doesn't play like that. God was there every inch of the way. He produces moments like that; we just have to step forward.

I drove home perplexed at my penchant for ignoring the truth. I was rehashing the conversation, and it hit me. God's grace is so encompassing it can swallow the likes of my father and me, regardless of what we had done to one another. We just need to listen and move.

Not too long ago, my wife, Diane, and I spent a weekend at my dad's place in Kentucky. It was the first time Diane met my father and stepmom. It was good, really good.

Rob was right. Fasting touches everyone around you.

I was watching my dad, my stepmom, and my wife talking, laughing, and having a great time. I was unbelievably happy at the prospect of all these new relationships. God's forgiveness was bearing itself out right in front of me. I didn't want to run. I was done hating my dad. I was done blaming him. I just wanted to love him. It was new and I liked it.

The fast was great, and Rob and I were forever changed. Changed because we didn't have to wonder anymore about where God was in our lives. He is always right in front of us. I put together a punch list of the things that happened during the forty days. It serves as a great reminder of the power of God.

Our faith was challenged.

Our study of the Bible took on necessity.

Our families were influenced by our actions.

We had daily conversations about faith.

We dropped 100 pounds between the two of us.

We watched our friends ask questions about Jesus.

We watched God heal my relationship with my father.

We watched our client base grow.

We watched as the Holy Spirit gave us words and power we never thought we had.

We watched our wives grow in their faith.

We watched Rob's kids grow in their faith.

Fasting is now a part of our lives. In 2005, Rob fasted a total of 105 days. I did 80. Fasting created the vehicle for which we gave our lives completely to God. Fasting reassured us of his power and grace. We do not ignore him anymore. We follow him.

My dad and I are going fishing soon.

JOHN 10:22-30   *Then came the Feast of Dedication at Jerusalem. It was winter, and Jesus was in the temple area walking in Solomon's Colonnade. The Jews gathered around him, saying, "How long will you keep us in suspense? If you are the Christ, tell us plainly."*

Jesus answered, "I did tell you, but you do not believe. The miracles I do in my Father's name speak for me, but you do not believe because you are not my sheep. My sheep listen to my voice; I know them, and they follow me. I give them eternal life, and they

*shall never perish; no one can snatch them out of my
hand. My Father, who has given them to me, is
greater than all; no one can snatch them out of my
Father's hand. I and the Father are one."*

It was late 2005, and God was telling me to take my family, pack them up, and get out of Dodge. I had been skipping around it for two months. When I would confront it, I sounded more like Magellan planning a trip than a guy who simply needed to listen to God. He was getting louder as I prayed. He was funny as he directed my attention to every House for Sale sign in town. He was not being definitive yet—a little annoying maybe, but not definitive.

5.7
ST. LOUIS TO
CHI-TOWN

J.R. and I fly a lot, and we're always complaining about cabin noise. The constant rattle and hum of the airplane. Bose invented the greatest thing for travelers: headphones that cancel out the cabin noise. Not since the Catalyst Conference has man been so blessed.

The second the cabin noise gets irritating, on go the headphones and peace is restored. The problem: You can't keep them on, because airlines have this thing about safety. Like takeoff and landing are sooo important. Apparently everyone needs instruction.

Anyway, Bose was rubbing off on me. I was taking the headphones into my life, replacing God's call for us to move with the justifications of everyday life. I'm too busy, my kids need this, and my wife has this going on. I have to pay this bill, please this guy and that guy. I was canceling out God. If it weren't for the preflight check and the landing instructions, I would have canceled myself right into a missed opportunity.

I was hitting my knees, halfheartedly asking God about this move. I had only one eye open. Hoping God would answer with Craig Gross in mind and not necessarily all things ministry. I can be selfish that way. I do have a significant track record with God. He has shown up big-time in my life, and for that I am extremely grateful. With that said, I do have that spiritual short-term memory loss thing. The kind of loss that will freak you out when things are changing in your life, yet you want control. You seem to forget there is an all-knowing, all-seeing, all-powerful God *living inside you,* very willing to help a brother out.

I was looking for information on our future move in sermons, radio preachers, TV pastors, MP3s, church Web sites—anywhere I thought I could find an answer. I was simply not listening to God. I was solely concerned with my own selfish position. The crazy thing about sin is that when we have a glimpse of the truth, we will always look for the easier, softer way to it. The easier, softer way is always paved with selfishness.

You want to know if you're listening to God? Ask yourself one question: *Who am I predominantly concerned with when I am making decisions?* Is it you and your plans? Is it God and his already-established will for you, found in his Word? It takes a lot of guts to answer this question. Answering means you will come face-to-face with yourself. If you are answering honestly, you will gain the understanding that your walk with Christ has very little to do with your plans and design. It is solely about serving God and those around you. That question should be in your breast pocket at all times. Use it as a guidepost for making decisions.

PROVERBS   *Does not wisdom call out?*
8:1-6   *Does not understanding raise her voice?*
            On the heights along the way,
                where the paths meet, she takes her stand;
                beside the gates leading into the city,
                at the entrances, she cries aloud:
            "To you, O men, I call out;
                I raise my voice to all mankind.
            You who are simple, gain prudence;
                you who are foolish, gain understanding.

Listen, for I have worthy things to say;
  I open my lips to speak what is right.

It was late November 2005, and I'd done a speaking gig
outside of St. Louis. I then had to drive to Chicago to meet
a friend. The trip takes about three hours, and it's nothing
but highway. I remember loading up the rental car, plot-
ting my conversation with God. I was ready for him to hear
me. I had waited three months for an answer—tonight he
was gonna tell me where we were going.

5.8
ALONE WITH
GOD

As I drove, I started talking to God. "Hey, I want this
drive to be you and me. Please tell me if I'm nuts or if you
really want us to move." I was pleading with him and getting nothing back. I was getting frustrated. I began to go
through all the scenarios in my head. Maybe we could
move to Oregon. Jeanette's family lives in Oregon; she
would love that. I like Nashville; it would be a great place
for the ministry. I really love Atlanta but hate the airport. I
was Magellan again, working it all out on my own.

Listen. Just listen to me, a small, quiet voice said.

I went silent. I turned off the radio and leaned back.

It took a few minutes ... I started to think about the place
that had been so good to XXXchurch.com during the four
years we had been up and running. The one place that sup-
ported us when we thought it might be over. That one
church that let us have a Sunday morning pulpit. That one
place that let us exercise our faith when the church wanted
nothing to do with us.

Mars Hill, that voice said. Now, I'm all for listening to
God, but Mars Hill Bible Church is in Grand Rapids, Michigan. Grand Rapids? I had been there before, and it was really cold. Like, three degrees.

"Come on!" my Southern Californian self said. "Grand
Rapids?"

Grand Rapids, that voice shot back. I sat in the dark,
cursing at seventy miles per hour. But then I got quiet,
peaceful. I began to really see it. This was a ministry move,

not a Craig Gross move. God was concerned with XXXchurch. Yes, he was going to take care of my wife, my kids, and me. I started to see a picture of a ministry growing and changing just as the people running it were. God was saying, *Go grow it.* Build it bigger, leaner, and in our world, meaner.

Cars and trucks were whipping by me. I wondered if the people passing by had the same thing going on in their vehicles, and if they did, whether God was being as patient with them as he was with me.

Chicago came quickly, and I felt like a weight had been lifted off my shoulders. God had laid it down, and the population of Grand Rapids was going to grow by four. I listened. He talked.

It's amazing how we push our agenda with him. We back God up against the walls of our lives. We tell him we need this or that. We give him deadlines. We are so used to living our lives instantly, right now, this second, immediately. We forget our lives are his. Not the other way around. Listening means we must be in a position to hear him.

5.9
MILE MARKER
47

On Thanksgiving weekend, my wife, Jeanette, and I were heading to visit some friends, and I had not yet said anything about the move. I was nervous, thinking perhaps I should have. She knew something was up and poked at me a little.

"Are you okay?" she asked.

"Yeah," I said, cool and calm while sweating Bibles. *What was I thinking? Moving? This is nuts!*

We were heading south from Riverside County to San Diego. I was watching the mile marker numbers getting higher, and I was about to explode. I was searching for the words. *How do I tell her without sounding nuts?* At mile marker 47, I blew:

"Jeanette, I need to say something."

My words were hurried and excited. I'd been married to Jeanette for seven years and had never been this nervous to talk to her. "Don't talk, so I can get this out. I've been praying a lot over the last few months, and God's been talking a lot. I think ... we're moving."

"*Moving?* Where?" she asked.

"Grand Rapids," I said with one eye on her and one eye on the road.

"Isn't Grand Rapids even farther away from my family?" she said with tears starting to come down her face. "You'd better keep praying."

Those tears brought the tension in the car to a stop. I went on to explain the last two months: "I didn't want to say anything, because I wasn't sure I was hearing it right," I said.

"It's cool," she said resignedly. "I knew something was going on." She sat calmly.

The single most important thing I have in this life is my wife, and right there, she got it. Got the call of God. Understood that listening to God means a lot of sacrifice at times.

The time passed quickly as we dreamed about what was ahead. We cried a little, laughed a little, dreamed a lot. Worried about selling our house, buying a new one. Leaving friends. Making new ones. It was a hurts-so-good kind of conversation.

This is what the Lord says: "When seventy years are completed for Babylon, I will come to you and fulfill my gracious promise to bring you back to this place. For I know the plans I have for you," declares the Lord, "plans to prosper you and not to harm you, plans to give you hope and a future."

JEREMIAH 29:10-11

God's plan for you, me, and the rest of humankind is real. He desires us to be near him and close to those who also know him, and always with a mind for those who need to be close to him.

5.10 ONE

One of the great things about God bringing us across the country was the reception we received from Mars Hill.

It was great watching all kinds of people come out of the woodwork to offer us everything from advice on winter coat buying to guided tours of the area. They made us feel like family. Family takes care of each other.

God's plan for us was simple. We needed to take this ministry and grow it. Not for our fame or glory, but for the guy or gal who is struggling. I moved XXXchurch.com halfway across the country. I took an antiporn ministry from the center of the porn world to Michigan. Michigan! Every time I say it, I laugh out loud. It sounds ridiculous. It makes absolutely no sense.

A lot about listening to God doesn't make sense. Having faith in something you have never seen, never heard, never touched. It's all quite nuts, except for the fact that your life changes on a dime when you engage Christ. When you listen and exercise that faith, the ignorable calling bears itself out in the fulfillment of your desires. God will fulfill the desires of your heart—that's the freedom you have as a result of Christ on the cross. You lose your life so you can find it, but you must listen and act.

God does have plans for you. Do you have plans for God? Are you placing yourself unreservedly in his care? Are you listening with honest ears? Are you making his plan your plan? All these questions are easy to ask, but answering them takes an incredible amount of faith. It means you must move, act, strike out, and tell the world how incredible Christ is. Tell them how you can't see him, feel him, or hear him, yet your life has changed because two thousand years ago some guy took the bullet for us all.

Dave the Horn Guy, J.R., me: We all have one thing in common. We are not great guys; we've got nothing new to add. We just stopped ignoring God, and we want you to know that you can too.

CHAPTER
IRREVERENT DEPENDENCY
6

CH 6 | IRREVERENT DEPENDENCY

He told them: "Take nothing for the journey—no LUKE 9:3-6
staff, no bag, no bread, no money, no extra tunic.
Whatever house you enter, stay there until you
leave that town. If people do not welcome you,
shake the dust off your feet when you leave their
town, as a testimony against them." So they set out
and went from village to village, preaching the
gospel and healing people everywhere.

J.R. and I would to like think we could travel without a 6.1
bag. Most likely we'd be crying the first night out. What NO BAG
if one of the disciples would have stepped up and said,
"Look, man, I have to have some clothes, toiletries, a
good book, and a magazine to make this trip"? That's
what goes through my mind. How did they follow so
blindly? How was it possible for men living in that time to
go from town to town and have nothing but the promise
of the Lord? It blows my mind the incredible faith these
guys all had. Luke 9 helps me step up my faith. It helps
me understand that my dependence on God needs to be
tested within those examples.

The Bible will set you up. You can get lost in its examples of faith and the lack thereof. Filled with irreverent
dependency, the Word smacks you with the existence of
men and women who run away from God and, in turn, directly into his arms. Irreverent dependency says you are
willing to stand on your own two feet when it comes to
acting out your faith.

Since the resurrection, the body of Christ has struggled
with its dependency on the cross. We try everything
within our reach to get closer to God, minus the Word.
That constant Christian searching away from the truth
spurs arguments and division. It's the lack of faith that

drives Christians insane with the possibilities of what is and what can be. We do a great job at the fight for God but stink when it comes to putting ourselves on the cross for our brothers.

You need to step up. Look at the excuses, look at the justifications, and look at the needs around you. Stop the irreverent dependency. Put down the life you think you need, and open yourself up to the life Christ has designed. You don't need a seminar, a class, a series, or even this book to learn what's going on in the Bible and exercise its examples in your life. Look at Luke 9 and do it. Take the Sermon on the Mount, and inject it into your life. Stop rallying the troops around your designs, and filter everything through someone else's needs.

LUKE 10:30-37   *In reply Jesus said: "A man was going down from Jerusalem to Jericho, when he fell into the hands of robbers. They stripped him of his clothes, beat him and went away, leaving him half dead. A priest happened to be going down the same road, and when he saw the man, he passed by on the other side. So too, a Levite, when he came to the place and saw him, passed by on the other side. But a Samaritan, as he traveled, came where the man was; and when he saw him, he took pity on him. He went to him and bandaged his wounds, pouring on oil and wine. Then he put the man on his own donkey, took him to an inn and took care of him. The next day he took out two silver coins and gave them to the innkeeper. 'Look after him,' he said, 'and when I return, I will reimburse you for any extra expense you may have.'*

Which of these three do you think was a neighbor to the man who fell into the hands of robbers?

The expert in the law replied, "The one who had mercy on him."

Jesus told him, "Go and do likewise."

The issue challenging the modern-day church is not the expression of faith—it's the exercising of political well-being. We are so comfortable lying to each other on Sundays, it feels like a scaled-down interim election. From the front row to the back row, Sunday mornings are filled with the worries of others. If we would step back and open our mouths every once in a while about the reality of our lives, we would come to the conclusion that it's okay to be flawed. Ultimately, churches need to challenge you to engage the world with your faith. We need to dress our salvation with the Word of God and act out our faith to whoever is within arm's reach.

We don't need door hangers, Starbucks outreaches, or once-a-quarter food drives. We need to be aware of the immediate, everyday needs of our community. This is the true jumping-off point for our faith. Christ healed people who didn't even ask to be healed. He understood immediate need. He understood the human condition physically and spiritually. He gave of himself until they killed him. His resurrection means you need to do the same.

Place yourself in front of some*one*, not some*thing*. Our Christian walk is "one to another" (James 5:16 KJV). When J.R. and I are on the road, we get one consistent question, and it's always whispered: "What can I do?"

The answer is easy to understand, but the most difficult thing you will ever be challenged with. Our answer is quite simple: Find the most needed thing in your community. Place yourself in front of people. Put yourself squarely in the middle of their lives. Does this mean homeless shelters, jails, hospitals, old folks' homes, orphanages, rehab facilities? Maybe. God will work out your passion.

When we speak to people about "immediate need," inevitably we hear, "God has not called me to anything yet." That sentence is possibly the most-ingested lie the Devil chucks at the world. People's immediate needs do not wrap themselves in nice little packages with pretty bows and easy-to-find solutions. We can't just send a check and hope things will be fine. We have to act. We have to step out in faith, grab another human being, and simply help.

What makes you stop and help an old lady cross a street? Or help the kid who fell on the playground? Or give your buddy fifty bucks for his rent? Why do you do it? What makes you help? The urging of the Holy Spirit is driving your need to help. Our problem is, we think that urging needs definition, but the only definition we should be concerned with are people's needs. If you're looking for God to tell you directly what to do, you are not studying the Word, and you're definitely not understanding that this ain't about you.

We struggle with this jumping-off point because we want the right scenario. We want *helping* to mean "convenience." We want quick, one-hour situations with no information exchanged. Why do you think car washes and walkathons are such popular fund-raisers? You get in and out, give your five bucks, and get home before dinner. We want it easy and clean; we really don't want anyone's problems.

"I'll give at the office."

"It's too dangerous."

"I can give an hour on Friday."

"Can't they go to a halfway house?"

"Doesn't the government have something set up for those people?"

This is how the immediate-need scenario usually plays out in our lives. As a result, we walk around with guilt and shame, always wondering when God will just tell us what to do. God has, in the form of people's immediate needs.

Getting involved with people's immediate needs will mean your life changes. It means you take a backseat. If you're asking, "What can I do?" God is saying, *Why can't you?* Your answer is where you find your heart.

Jesus answered her, "If you knew the gift of God   JOHN 4:10
and who it is that asks you for a drink, you would
have asked him and he would have given you living
water."

Almost immediately after Hurricane Katrina made landfall,   6.3
the images of the fallout hit TV, and it was bad. Remem-   ONE FAMILY
ber? Unbelievable destruction. From houses to people, it
was horrible. I remember sitting with Di on the couch, crying, watching it live, as people were desperately waving
down helicopters to come rescue them. It broke my heart.
Interview after interview, it was clear: Thousands of people had lost everything, and they were all in need.

I could hear the Holy Spirit calling inside of me, *Do
something.* Without a helicopter and some kind of hover-
craft, I had no idea, other than to send money to the
many relief agencies. I went online and started to see a
groundswell of activity. Churches were taking in families
and creating bulletin boards with people's information,
hoping others would take in a family. Families were being
relocated all over the country. A woman from Hawaii took
a family—it was incredible to watch.

Diane and I have no kids. After twelve years of marriage and a whole lot of trying, the doctors told us, "It's
not gonna happen." Di was devastated to say the least.
Everyone around us said, "Just go adopt. It will be all
right." We actually mourned a child we would never have.
It sucked.

Di and I have this joke when people ask about kids: We
tell them we live with two dogs and a guy named Bore-
dom. People who have kids just smile; they don't really
get it. People who are in our situation laugh out loud.
When you don't have kids, it can get really quiet and un-
eventful. Both of our extended families are filled with
kids, and we adore every waking minute with them. For
us, our nephews and nieces are our kids.

So here we were with two empty bedrooms and the

largest national disaster in this country's history. It was easy for us. I turned to Di and said, "Let's do it. Let's get a family up here."

She hesitantly said, "What are you planning?"

"We've got the room; let's get a family up here." After a good long talk we agreed to do it.

Among our supporters at XXXchurch.com, one of the best has to be Integrity Online. They are an Internet-filtering company based in Alabama. The head guy is Skip Matthews, a guy with enough southern drawl to go around. He is kind, considerate, and always straightforward. It's refreshing. Skip was right in the path of Hurricane Katrina, so right away, I e-mailed him to make sure things were okay. Skip wrote back quickly. Given the circumstances, I was shocked to hear from him so rapidly. Skip wrote, "Although things are very bad, everyone at Integrity is fine, and it will take awhile to get back up to normal." I was relieved everyone was fine. I wrote back and told him if he needed anything, please let me know.

A day or two later, the Holy Spirit was still banging on me about the people in New Orleans. I popped open the laptop and wrote Skip again, this time asking if he knew any families that needed temporary housing. Within the day, he got back with a very definitive "YES!" Skip asked me for my information and who I thought would be a good fit for us. I responded that we had room for four people: maybe mom, dad, two kids. Skip took the info and posted it on a community board at his church. At the time, his church had taken in several families displaced by the storm.

That weekend, Di was having a garage sale, and the usual suspects were showing up to look at the junk: neighbors, family, good friends. The conversations all day were geared around New Orleans. Everyone agreed it was horrible. Everyone agreed the people in New Orleans needed prayer and a lot of support in the upcoming months. But something very strange happened when we announced our plans to bring a family to our little farm-house outside of Cleveland. It got quiet. Very quiet. The silence took us aback a little. These people standing in the midst of our junk were people we genuinely love and admire. One by one, these people killed the idea.

"You have to be very careful with these decisions," one said.

"Are you sure you know what you're doing?"

"Did you pray about this?"

"You have valuables in your house."

"Valuables?" I said out loud. "What do valuables have to do with this?"

"They might rob you," someone said. "They might hurt you and Diane. You don't know what they will do."

"Well," Diane said, wanting to break the tension. "Any-one want coffee?"

I was standing on the edge of one of the most selfless things I had ever wanted to do, and the seeds of doubt and fear had just been firmly planted.

I was in my head all night. Thinking over and over again about Diane and her safety. I was thinking through all the scenarios. What if these people were not responsible? What if they were violent? What if they did steal my stuff? What if they did hurt us? What if, what if, what if … I "what if'd" myself to sleep.

Jesus said, "Feed my sheep. I tell you the truth, *when you were younger you dressed yourself and* *went where you wanted; but when you are old you* *will stretch out your hands, and someone else will* *dress you and lead you where you do not want to* *go."*

JOHN 21:17-18

Skip called bright and early on Monday. "J.R., I have great news! Looks like we have a family."

"Let's hear it," I said.

6.4
"I'LL CALL HIM TODAY"

"Well, it's a couple. They are not married, but they were planning it before the hurricane hit. They have two kids and are ready to relocate." Skip was excited. I could tell he had done his best at hooking this up, finding the right fit. We talked for about ten minutes.

The couple sounded great: He worked for the phone company, and she was in the restaurant business. The kids were in grade school. I was excited, and Skip was good in helping me understand this was a big step. "You have to listen to God, J.R.," he said with his cool southern accent. "You have to do what is right for your family. This is a big deal if you do it," he said. "The guy's name is David. Give him a call today."

Di and I talked for a long time after Skip called. I rolled out my worry about safety and not knowing these people. The garage sale hypocrites had planted the doubt, and it was growing prolifically; I was now spreading the disease to Diane, and she heard me loud and clear.

"I never thought of that," she said, a little horrified that these people might be capable of very bad things.

"I know. We don't know. We just don't know," I said, afraid of what I had set in motion.

We knew God was telling us to do it. We had prayed about this, talked about it, even sought counsel. Di and I had taken giant steps of faith before, mostly designed around switching jobs or moving to a new city, and this was a step of faith that looked easy. We had the room and the means to help other people.

People. That was ultimately the problem: These were human beings, not jobs or cities. These were human beings, with real, 24/7 needs and emotions. These were folks who were so different from us in so many ways. From race to religion, there was so much we didn't know and understand. Fear and doubt began to replace our faith. These people were suffering, and I began to recoil like the hypocrite I am.

That afternoon, I hovered over my phone, trying to

summon up the courage to call this man who needed me. Finally, about three o'clock, I dialed. A deep, low, friendly sounding voice answered, "Hello."

"Hi … David? It's J.R. Mahon from Cleveland. How are things going?" Stupid question. I knew how things were going.

"Well, not so good," David said. "I'm trying to get out of this state and relocate my family."

"What are the short-term plans?" I asked.

"We just want a clean start at this point," he replied. "We've lost everything. The only thing I have left is my car, that's it. And some clothes for the kids."

"Is the church taking good care of you?" I asked.

"Oh yeah, the kids are playing and we're being fed, it's all good. We just want to get out of here."

It was clear the family had been shell-shocked, and the only thing that made sense was starting new somewhere else. I was desperately trying to read this guy. I needed something—anything—to let me know he was on the level. I was fishing, and it made me sick. This guy had lost everything and wanted his family safe and back to normal, and here I was playing Columbo, looking for any flaw so I could say, "Yeah, this isn't gonna work."

I was a man without God.

I told David I needed to talk things over with my wife and that I would call him back within the next couple of days. He said, "Thanks for calling." I wished him luck and hung up.

After I hung up, it was clear—I was not going to do this. I let the doubt and fear ride so heavily on this decision; it was over. I literally turned my back. I was now dealing with this family solely based on *my* comfort and not *their* immediate need. I left discernment on the table. I let God know exactly where I was living. I passed on helping another human being.

I became so ultra-aware of my sin over the next few days, it was as if the Holy Spirit plugged an amplifier into my brain. I justified every move I was making. It all sounded so nice. My sin started making sense as I told myself this is not the will of God because ... because ... because ... because ...

If I am honest with you, and believe me, this is not easy, I didn't do it because I would be displaced. I didn't do it because it meant my comfort would be displaced. It meant my everyday routine would be displaced. It meant giving something up for someone else, and I couldn't do it. Christ saved my life, and there I was staring the very act of love in the face, and I ran and hid.

I have a hard time even looking at this page.

I called David a couple of days later and told him it just wasn't going to work. You ever bold-faced lied to someone who desperately needs your help? I have. A day does not go by since talking to David that I don't think about him, pray about him, and regret what I did. It took a few months for the truth to surface in my life. I would wander through the Bible and see David's need all over the place. I would pray, and God would tap on my conscience and ask if anyone was home. It hit like a slow-moving avalanche. My dependency on God stopped for my own selfish desire. I have not, to this day, contacted David, and again it is one of the worst single events in my life. Hurricane Katrina became a lesson in not acting out sin.

Whose immediate need are you running from? Whose life can you change by giving your time? We all have stuff going on; we are all tied to this or that. We must ingest the idea of Christ's sacrifice for our everyday existence. We are not here for ourselves; we are here for families like David's, or even the guy across the street who just waves every now and then.

JOB 42:1-6   *Then Job replied to the Lord:*

"I know that you can do all things;
*   no plan of yours can be thwarted.*

You asked, 'Who is this that obscures my counsel
    without knowledge?'
Surely I spoke of things I did not understand,
    things too wonderful for me to know.

"You said, 'Listen now, and I will speak;
    I will question you,
    and you shall answer me.'
My ears had heard of you
    but now my eyes have seen you.
Therefore I despise myself
    and repent in dust and ashes."

Job was beaten on, down and out. If I'd gone through what he'd gone through, I would have caved. I would have found the highest mountain, climbed it, gotten a rock, and thrown it at God. Job maintained. He lost everything dear to him, including his health. He cursed the day he was born and wanted to know why, yet he knew beneath all the anger and suffering that his deliverance would be found through his pain. Given the circumstances, Job had an amazing amount of faith and dependence.

6.5
"HE CAN'T
FEEL
ANYTHING"

God did have answers for Job—not the typical church answers we'd expect for a guy who just got the stuffing knocked out of him. God said, "See all this around you? It's all mine. I created it, all of it, and I will do with it whatever I like. You and anyone else walking around should really understand: It's all mine. I decide. Not you—me." God answered deliberately and forcefully. He's God. Job was boiled down and given an incredible opportunity to lie flat before God and "get it." Get that God created it and will take care of it. No matter the circumstances. Job remained faithful and dependent on God and was blessed twice as much as he had been (see Job 42:10).

I try really hard to wrap my head around what God was thinking. Why would God take a blameless man and hand him over to the Devil? (Job 1:6–12; 2:3–6). Why would he watch as Job suffered so terribly and not give him rest? Why did the torture continue so others could see it, and why, when it was all said and done, did God simply assert himself as Creator?

My mindless conclusions about Job couldn't fill a thimble, but a part of me knows God let it all go down so you and I would know that dependence and faith should never hinge on mitigating circumstances. We can lose it all, and God will still be God. Did you get that? God will still be God. Write that on the cleanest wall in your house: God will always be God.

It was hard for my family to leave Tides Church, our congregation in California. My wife and I had grown roots there. We simply loved the people at Tides. The senior pastor, Bryan, is a great guy, always smiling, always ready to give someone a hand. The church was filled with people like Bryan who were always ready to help.

I travel much of the time, and most Sundays I am unable to get to services at Tides, so Bryan and I started a small group at my house on Monday nights. No one really came to it, because, well, who wants to hang with the lead pastor and the porn pastor? Most Monday nights it would be just Bryan's family and my family. Over the past year we all became pretty close. I would tell him about XXXchurch, and he would fill me in on the haps at Tides. Sort of a ministry accountability partnership.

I was in Cleveland one weekend with J.R. and the wives. J.R. can't stand chain restaurants and I love them, so I tortured him at Bahamas Breeze. We were about ten minutes into some good spinach dip with island chips and Jamaican grilled chicken wings when Jeanette's phone rang.

"Hello?!" (Jeanette always answers happily.) Her expression quickly changed, though—it was clear the person on the other side of that phone call had bad news. Jeanette's face got very serious. "Okay ... okay ... okay," she said.

"Who is it?" I asked as I gave her the "tell me now" finger.

She covered up the phone and quickly said, "Bryan was in an accident, and it's not so good."

I panicked. So did the rest of the table.

Jeanette ended the call with "Let him know we are praying for him." It's never good when you hear that. Jeanette hung up, and the volley of questions started:

"What happened?"

"Is he okay?"

"Was it a car accident?"

"Was that his wife?"

Jeanette sat back in the booth and said, "Bryan was off-loading the new staging for the church, and nine hundred pounds of metal staging fell and crushed him to the ground."

That weekend, Tides was moving into Lakeside High School in Lake Elsinore, California, and one of the last elements to be delivered was the stage. The delivery company had asked Bryan to help take it off the truck. As he was working inside the truck, the delivery guy was outside. The staging slipped, and in a split second, hundreds of pounds of metal came loose from the bed of the truck and fell directly on top of Bryan.

Bryan tried to duck and cover his head, but it was too late. The staging crushed the back of his head, pushing it forward, all the way into his chest. Bryan immediately lost all feeling in his arms and legs.

In an instant, Bryan had become a quadriplegic.

His mom was with him and went into an immediate panic. Lying on the bed of the truck, Bryan tried to calm his mom down and assure her he would be okay. Minutes later, Bryan was taken by ambulance to the hospital. Upon arrival, he was airlifted to Loma Linda and told he would probably never walk again.

Needless to say, the jerk chicken lost its taste after that call. We prayed quickly, finished dinner, and went home, frightened for our friend.

Starving Jesus

MATTHEW
6:25-34

Therefore I tell you, do not worry about your life, what you will eat or drink; or about your body, what you will wear. Is not life more important than food, and the body more important than clothes? Look at the birds of the air; they do not sow or reap or store away in barns, and yet your heavenly Father feeds them. Are you not much more valuable than they? Who of you by worrying can add a single hour to his life?

And why do you worry about clothes? See how the lilies of the field grow. They do not labor or spin. Yet I tell you that not even Solomon in all his splendor was dressed like one of these. If that is how God clothes the grass of the field, which is here today and tomorrow is thrown into the fire, will he not much more clothe you, O you of little faith? So do not worry, saying, "What shall we eat?" or "What shall we drink?" or "What shall we wear?" For the pagans run after all these things, and your heavenly Father knows that you need them. But seek first his kingdom and his righteousness, and all these things will be given to you as well. Therefore do not worry about tomorrow, for tomorrow will worry about itself. Each day has enough trouble of its own.

Bryan's neck suffered the most damage, and the doctors calmly explained that he would need surgery and many hours of painful rehabilitation.

The members of Tides Church turned out in force. Other churches turned out in force. People were stepping up for Bryan, his wife, and their two kids. It was great to watch a rallying point for the church. People were praying for Bryan, giving their time, cooking for the family, helping with the household and finances.

Meanwhile, I was worrying about Bryan. I almost couldn't help it. My mind was nuts with the "what ifs":

What if the doctor botches the surgery?

What if he stays paralyzed?

What if he goes broke?

What if Tides Church goes under?

I was living with irreverent dependency on God. My mind and spirit were distracted with the causes and conditions of my own logic and sense. Not once did I pull my head up and away from the worry and try to understand that God would always be God. Bryan needed me to stand with him faithfully. Bryan didn't need another detractor from the reality of his paralysis; he needed people willing to dig down deep in faith. Bryan needed big faith, big dependence; and he needed it in the form of others around him encouraging him to continue looking at God, not asking, "Why?" but "What's next?"

The body of Christ is lost in its exclusivity. Sometimes. We miss opportunities like Bryan's. We rally the troops with cards, letters, and prayers, not realizing the cards, letters, and prayers should never stop. Bryan, his family, and our congregation had to come to the foot of the cross. We were forced to find God in our daily lives because a pastor tried to unload staging. We were forced to faithfully consider our dependence on God.

The church often isolates these stories simply as examples of faith. I would submit that these stories are God being God. He is demanding our attention, our time, and our faith. He needs us not to worry, not to take matters into our own hands. He simply wants us to draw closer to him. We should embrace the immediate needs of others as our exercise in faith and dependence. Encourage others to bear the weight of hard times through faith and action. Give God the opportunity to bless your life based on your choice to follow him.

Surgery and prayers seem to go hand in hand; sometimes the body of Christ needs a scalpel to draw us to our knees. For weeks, Bryan and the doctors really didn't know how it was going to shake out. He went through periods of intense pain. He had problems with his feeding tube and had to pass a swallow evaluation in order to eat Jell-O. Doctors fused a few vertebrae together, and it was extremely painful. Bryan has always been that guy you rely on; he was the helper, not the helped. It was incredibly hard for Bryan to be sidelined and let this play out.

Bryan was being put to the test and was answering back with nothing but praise for what God was doing. It was amazing to watch as he and his wife ran with this as if they had done it before. It became clear that nothing would stop this couple from making a full recovery and letting everyone know it was God who needed all the glory. He slowly regained feeling in his arms and legs. The doctors were skeptical, saying thing like "You will probably never have the full use of your legs." Some even said, "The reality is you will never be the same."

True. At least not spiritually.

The staging had been put up. The new services rolled out in the high school. Tides Church was moving forward, and the lead pastor was stashed away in a hospital room far away from all the action. It started to take on that "only God could do this" feel and look.

The church saw significant growth during the time Bryan was laid up. Bryan was able to keep up with the day-to-day from his hospital bed. From conference calls to late-night hospital visits, things moved forward at Tides regardless of his physical immobility. Attendance shot through the roof as the community watched a church rally around an all-knowing, all-powerful God in the form of a partially paralyzed pastor. It was amazing to go to church and see new people who were identifying with a guy they had never met. Bryan's paralysis moved people to church.

His recovery was slow but sure, and thirty-six days (yes, thirty-six days—after the accident), Bryan walked (yes, Bryan walked) out of that hospital and into the arms of a grateful and inspired community. His wife, his kids, and all the rest of us who called Tides Church home welcomed him back and praised God for the work he had done. Bryan had one thing to say: "Thank you!"

Bryan wrote everyone a letter and posted it on the Tides Web site:

3/16

Before I was airlifted to Loma Linda, while I was still on the ground at Inland Valley, I saw the number 7 above my bed: the number that always adorned my Little League jersey and e-mail accounts. I learned long ago as a child the number was God's, and it meant "completion." "Thank you, God," I said out loud. I knew from that moment on that God was going to bring me to a place of completion!

I saw the number several more times as the days went slowly by. My surgery was at 7 a.m. The surgery was 7 hours long on the 7th of October. My recovery room was number 7. I was in a 7th Day Adventist hospital! On my second stay, I was admitted into room number 12 (I was crushed); however, I soon learned not to fear as I was on floor number 7!!! Completion!!!!! God's desire for you and for me.

While I still have a way to go, I am progressing continually! I want to take this time to thank all of you who have and are continuing to pray for me. For those who sent flowers and cards too many to name. For the many visits and repeat visits (I know it was a haul to get out there) from so many of you. For those who stepped up in my stead so that I could enjoy my vacation.

Thanks to my staff! Thanks, D.J., Paul, Ken, Mark, Tracy, Fish, Tamara, and Bryan. You guys really stepped it up and inspired our church to new heights. To our congregation, you ROCK! Our church has seen explosive growth because our community has seen what it means for a church to be a family! What a testimony you have shown the city of Lake Elsinore.

In May I have been asked to share my story with the rest of the city officials and spiritual leaders in our community at the mayor's prayer breakfast. I know God will continue to do great things because of this great thing that He has done!

As the days and months go by, please continue to pray for my family and me as I continue to heal. Deb is doing well and slowly letting me handle money again (hee hee). The boys are growing and demanding all of our attention, and we love it—especially me!!!

God bless you all!! God has truly done a miracle, and He will not stop His work in us until we are all Complete in Him.

—Pastor Bryan

JOB 42:16-17 *After this, Job lived a hundred and forty years; he saw his children and their children to the fourth generation. And so he died, old and full of years.*

6.6
THAT ONE
THREAD

I love imagining Job living out his years, sitting back in a big comfortable chair, waxing poetic about the time he had sores all over his body and had lost everything. How he talked to the Lord and how the Lord talked back. People would listen, shake their heads, and say, "That's the craziest thing I have ever heard." Some would ask Job to share his story at local services. Some would encourage him to shop his story to Zondervan. Others would ask him to come speak at their companies to inspire the employees. Job would soon have his own DVD set, book deals, Youth Specialties main stage appearances. *Relevant* magazine would put him in every issue for a year and hope Bono would understand there's a new guy in town. Jerry Falwell would have to ignore it as a passing fad.

It's a story we always go back to. It's that one thread we hold on to when something sucks. When our lives have developed a cancer, when our faith seems too far from right. We look back, way back, to a sore-covered body. A man seemingly without God. We then look up and say, "Thank you." Irreverent dependency looks like a broken Etch A Sketch. Its lines blur quickly on every issue in our lives. We forgo God's calling for our own immediate comfort. Job locked himself in on the pain and offered up his life to God until the Lord himself answered. The Devil didn't answer; the Lord did. God spoke to Job and said, "Job, I'm all you need," and Job got it.

Find that person you can't love and make the effort. Find that spot that stretches you so much it hurts and go for it. Step over your comfort and experience someone else's immediate need. Tell them it's going to be okay because you get it. Because you just want to love them. I don't know what that looks like for you. Maybe it's a "hello" at the store, maybe it's taking in a family who needs a place to stay. Or maybe it's your simple acknowledgment that God is all you need.

CH 7 | SHORT OF SIN

Therefore, I urge you, brothers, in view of God's ROMANS 12:1-8
mercy, to offer your bodies as living sacrifices,
holy and pleasing to God—this is your spiritual act
of worship. Do not conform any longer to the
pattern of this world, but be transformed by the
renewing of your mind. Then you will be able to
test and approve what God's will is—his good,
pleasing and perfect will.

For by the grace given me I say to every one of
you: Do not think of yourself more highly than you
ought, but rather think of yourself with sober
judgment, in accordance with the measure of faith
God has given you. Just as each of us has one
body with many members, and these members do
not all have the same function, so in Christ we
who are many form one body, and each member
belongs to all the others. We have different gifts,
according to the grace given us. If a man's gift is
prophesying, let him use it in proportion to his
faith. If it is serving, let him serve; if it is teaching,
let him teach; if it is encouraging, let him encour-
age; if it is contributing to the needs of others, let
him give generously; if it is leadership, let him
govern diligently; if it is showing mercy, let him do
it cheerfully.

This book, *Starving Jesus*, is a natural extension of our 7.1
faith. J.R. and I have grown into this. It is imperative for us OPPORTUNITY
to share Christ with the world. This ain't the parking lot
ministry. It took us awhile, but we finally accepted our
place as disciples.

Starving Jesus is a call. If you are struggling with what to
do in the name of Christ, here is the opportunity. This is an

opportunity to create something, to turn nothing into some-thing. It doesn't have to be a worldwide ministry with your own jet and million-dollar donors (although if it happens, call us). We are suggesting becoming outrageous, experimental, entrepreneurial, and bold. We are steadfast with the idea of anything short of sin to drive the message of Christ into the world.

We take a lot of heat for dealing with off-the-map sub-jects. This book will no doubt see its share of people who hate the title and its message. The overwhelming major-ity of those people will be Bible-carrying Christians. Dealing with "Christian hate" is a part of our lives. We re-ceive e-mails from so-called Christians who doom us to hell and hope our outreaches fail miserably. We get phone calls from Christians so irate that they have a hard time breathing as they yell at us. We are no strangers to controversy, and we have no problem sitting in the mid-dle of it. Some say we are seeking the spotlight. Others think we are publicity whores.

The truth about us is simple: We love Christ and believe passionately in spreading the gospel to the lost and sick. Hard to believe when we work for a ministry called XXXchurch.com and drive a Porn Mobile. Hard to believe when we go to porn shows and proclaim Jesus Christ is Savior. Hard to believe when we write a book saying the American body of Christ is not getting it done.

We want to attract the attention of the world with the message about Christ. We will be outrageous. We will think about the media impact of our events. We will tell you over and over again that Jesus Christ is your bridge to God the Father. That's it. As a friend of mine loves to say, "Those who complain do not create."

1 TIMOTHY
6:11-16

But you, man of God, flee from all this, and pursue righteousness, godliness, faith, love, endurance and gentleness. Fight the good fight of the faith. Take hold of the eternal life to which you were called

when you made your good confession in the pres-
ence of many witnesses. In the sight of God, who
gives life to everything, and of Christ Jesus, who
while testifying before Pontius Pilate made the good
confession, I charge you to keep this command
without spot or blame until the appearing of our
Lord Jesus Christ, which God will bring about in his
own time—God, the blessed and only Ruler, the King
of kings and Lord of lords, who alone is immortal
and who lives in unapproachable light, whom no one
has seen or can see. To him be honor and might for-
ever. Amen.

7.2
I LOOKED FOR
A TREE

I was in the middle of the newsroom, wondering what I was doing. I had been in this place a million times before. The pressure of an impossible deadline, hundreds of decisions to make within the hour. Reporters hating shooters. Shooters hating reporters. Producers hating me. It was all in the name of a great television career. I snapped the orders, my voice loud and clear. Everyone scrambled, and the work of putting on a local news show commenced. I sat back at my desk, empty. The lack of Christ in my decision making had me running hard.

I worked in local TV for about twenty years, wearing several hats, from photojournalist to executive producer. Television came easy; it has always been the one thing I know I do very well, from the physical act of putting something on TV to understanding why and how people watch. I was born with a great deal of discernment, which, if used in the TV business, meant I had an easy time understanding audiences. That talent, if you will, is a gold mine for networks and local stations across the country. The more you understand viewing habits, the better chance you have of increasing your ratings, which leads to cold hard cash in advertising. I was good at TV.

Over the years, my hard work paid off. I was handed great opportunities in the television business, which got me everything I thought I needed to live a long and happy life. Great cars, great homes, vacations in the Caribbean, front-row seats at concerts and sporting events, money, power, and the luxury to use TV as my personal soapbox. An entire city at my beck and call. It was fun, to say the least. I won awards, received the accolades of my peers, traveled the world ... and fell in love with myself.

One of the perks of the world is a selfish love that can transcend the love of others, leaving you helplessly devoted to yourself. You get so lost in your selfish desires outside of faith that you become powerless to love and receive love. Look around you. You will find people so lost in selfish ends they have forgotten how to love and receive love. It's a sad way to live, but the world rewards it.

It rewarded me, and I ate it up. "Look at me!" I shouted. "Look how great my talent is; look how much I know!" All the time ignoring the call of God. In the end, everyone around me was sick of me, and I was sick of myself. A head full of Christ and a heart filled with earthly desires equals death. I had stopped caring about people.

That afternoon, standing in the newsroom, I realized it was all for nothing. I grabbed my coat and headed for the door. I was done. My television career was over. My mindless decisions to air out the trappings of the world on TV were over. I was adding nothing to the kingdom of God and being rewarded for it. I caught my reflection in the car window; I didn't understand who I had become. Was I the guy pulling the trigger on airing murders and celebrity gossip for your entertainment? Or was I a disciple of Christ? The answer was clear. Like Judas, I looked for a tree.

LUKE 5:27-28   *After this, Jesus went out and saw a tax collector by the name of Levi sitting at his tax booth. "Follow me," Jesus said to him, and Levi got up, left everything and followed him.*

I sat in my dining room, exhausted from being without God
for so long. I was about to throw $100,000 a year out the
window because I was going to follow Jesus. Nuts, absolutely nuts. I had great benefits, the perks of being an
executive producer. I was firmly planted in the world. I had
worked my butt off to get these things, and now I wanted
to follow Jesus.... I couldn't help laughing at myself, because nothing made more sense. It was insane. I had very
little in my 401(k), no savings, no stocks, no bonds. I was
broke without my job and sitting on a butt-load of debt.
Leaving looked like the most incredibly irresponsible, stupid thing a human being could do. It made no worldly
sense, none! Yet a feeling of peace was on me like a warm
summer night.

Diane and I talked throughout that afternoon. She was
looking me dead in the face and saying very clearly, "Do
it!" She understood, perhaps more than me, it sometimes
takes a radical amputation to get on with the business of
living for God. She was strong, unflinching. She had a con-
fidence that put me at ease: "It will be okay, baby. God will
take care of us."

What was going on? Part of me was leaving and I didn't
care. All the things I was taught to respect while growing
up, I was chucking. The money, security, and success were
leaving me as fast as I could think. Within one afternoon,
I had given up, surrendered my life to Christ. I was prepared to do anything short of sin to step over the line and
follow him. I had to. I could not face God anymore knowing I was willingly living outside his call in my life.

I opened my laptop, wrote my resignation letter, drove
it down to the station, put it on the boss's desk, and called
it a day. I had prayed for that moment a thousand times.

Large crowds were traveling with Jesus, and turn-   LUKE 14:25-30
ing to them he said: "If anyone comes to me and
does not hate his father and mother, his wife and

children, his brothers and sisters—yes, even his own life—he cannot be my disciple. And anyone who does not carry his cross and follow me cannot be my disciple.

Suppose one of you wants to build a tower. Will he not first sit down and estimate the cost to see if he has enough money to complete it? For if he lays the foundation and is not able to finish it, everyone who sees it will ridicule him, saying, 'This fellow began to build and was not able to finish.'"

**7.4
MY HOME**

My story is not new to the Christian landscape. I know hundreds of men and women who have made the same jump, who left all the crap of the world to follow Jesus. I am not the first to flip out and bail. I will not be the last.

In my case, discipleship meant losing my job, cashing out my 401(k), and praying a lot. Mostly losing my life. I had just left all the worldly security I had ever known. I had no idea what I was doing. I had the Bible and its examples of faith. I had the support of my loving wife, who stood strong, right next to me, and said, "Do it. Be the man you have always wanted to be." That's it. I think we had $1,500 in the bank. I had a $1,200-a-month mortgage payment and monthly bills that totaled about $4,000. My faith was right in front of me, and I was scared out of my mind. It didn't feel like this when I quit my job—in fact, quite the opposite. Here I was, jobless, with no money, and the Lord's promise that he would take care of me. What was I thinking?

The body of Christ sees radical change as isolated and a bit on the edge. When they find out little Johnny has flipped out in the name of the Lord, it scares them. I wandered around for fifteen years as a Christian looking for that magic bullet that would get me squarely in front of Christ, but I didn't find it in the pulpit or a Bible study.

The bullet came in the form of my disobedience. I sold out for Christ, because I had no choice. It was either die

Born Again Lazy or live for Christ. Immediately, the world reacted with a resounding "J.R. has flipped out. He went nuts." Our cute little Christian subculture took a step back and wanted to know if I had truly heard from God. It was amazing: The very people who told me over and over again to follow Christ questioned and, in some cases, opposed my radical step of faith.

It was inconceivable to some that I left the paycheck, the security of a company that gave me free dental and life insurance. They cared very little about my full conversion. They just wanted me to keep quiet about what it looked like, which looked like a guy making bad decisions. It looked like I was willingly screwing up my life. It looked radical, edgy. It scared people who clung to the notion that American Christianity is wrapped up in a good paycheck, benefits, a nice home, and a Starbucks gift card in the wallet.

I didn't count on church fear. The body of Christ is afraid of disciples outside their circle of influence. I understood the world's reaction to my craziness—but the church's? The ink on my resignation letter hadn't dried yet, and the phone calls came in making sure I was "okay." Okay? I was running straight into the arms of God. What I had done made no sense to those without a relationship with Christ. That I understood. But for those wearing crosses around their necks and preaching on Sundays, shame on them for giving the gospel of Christ a statute of limitations.

The conversation about my situation became curiosity for the world and judgmental deliberation for the church. The world chalked it up to premidlife crisis, and the body of Christ held up a microscope, trying to find the Devil.

I didn't look back after the jump. To bring in money, I took some freelance gigs producing industrial videos. My focus stayed clear: Live life as a disciple. In the fall of 2002, which was during my first year out on my own, God gave me a unique vision for a business/ministry that would cater to the creative needs of ministries. Sort of an advertising agency for God. My good friend Rob Supan would also make the jump and join me. Together we started Gate Creative. Rob became the creative director and, ultimately, the CEO of Gate.

Rob and I never saw it coming. God showed up the day we hung the shingle out front. Gate exploded with work. Web sites, marketing plans, national image campaigns. God used every fiber of our beings to move the gospel. He gave us work, paid our bills, and took care of our families. We were grateful for every day. Rob and I grew to be best friends as we created our own rhetoric for what Gate is and will be. We built something from nothing, and God has received all the glory.

In the first year, Gate helped plant six churches and launched a national campaign called Porn Sunday with XXXchurch.com. If you had told me the day I handed in my resignation I would be working with something called XXXchurch.com, I would have asked, "What have you been smoking?"

We slowed down periodically and looked around at the incredible things going on. I was finally racking up some solid history with God—the kind of history that says he is real. Before that time, my life had been a carnival shooting game in which I was constantly missing the target. I relied so much on myself that God was always a second thought. Taking up the cross meant I had to find him, no matter what. I was cornered by him to do whatever was in front of me. That first year of Gate Creative's life, I prayed more, fasted more, and gave more than I had during my entire Christian walk. It was amazing seeing fruit come out of our little office outside of Cleveland, Ohio. God was providing, and we were in awe of him. He really was real. I say that as if I don't believe in him, because sometimes I don't.

Toward the end of that first year, I was invited to a porn convention with XXXchurch.com. The plan for me was to help with the outreach on the showroom floor. I was willing and intrigued. I talked to Diane and Rob, and it was clear I should go. The show would become bittersweet for me, as it wound up ending my involvement with Gate Creative.

I arrived at the show full of expectations as to what it would look like, smell like, and feel like. I worried about falling into temptation; I worried about what people would think of me. I worried I would not have the right words. I worried no one would listen to the words I did have.

The convention was the biggest amassed venue for sinful behavior I had ever seen. Incredible sin on display. I quickly understood why it was so important to be a light in there. It changed me. I was willing to do anything short of sin and found myself at one of the world's largest adult expos: Erotica LA.

The convention taught me more about God in two days than the church had in almost twenty years. I couldn't believe it. God was right in front of me, and he was speaking so clearly it frightened me. *J.R., here they are. People my Son died for. Please tell them about me; love them. Help them hear my voice. Help them know me. Do not judge them; tell them Christ died for their sins.*

It was the best thing I had ever done. I had boundless energy, and the Holy Spirit gave me words I didn't know I had. I felt more comfortable there than I had ever felt in any church. Around me were ten other people who believed just as I did. I prayed with people right there on the porn-show floor. I read the Bible with people—at the porn show! I had hundreds of conversations about Christ. I witnessed more than I had in two years.

The show cemented me in ministry. God had showed me another door, and without even realizing it, I ran through. I was spinning from all the conversations, all the needs, and all the people who needed Christ. We talked to thousands of porn-hungry folks who wanted to talk about God. There was no arguing or debating—just us in a ten-foot-by-ten-foot booth, asking one question: "Who do you think

Christ is?" We connected with folks, got e-mail addresses and phone numbers. Relationships were started and common ground was found. All because we were willing to do anything short of sin.

The last night of the show, Craig and I went across the street to grab a late dinner, and Craig looked at me and smiled.

"What?" I said.

"What did you think?" He knew what had happened to me during the last three days. The same thing happened to him a few years earlier at the Las Vegas show. I knew what he was asking.

"About what?" I asked.

"The show!" he shot back.

I sat back in the chair and, as well meaning as I could be, I said, "I will never just sit in a pew again."

PROVERBS
16:1-4

To man belong the plans of the heart,
    but from the Lord comes the reply of the tongue.
All a man's ways seem innocent to him,
    but motives are weighed by the Lord.
Commit to the Lord whatever you do,
    and your plans will succeed.
The Lord works out everything for his own ends—
    even the wicked for a day of disaster.

7.5
I DIDN'T ASK
FOR IT

I sat in the Gate office with the truth crawling up my spine. I was scared—almost unbearably so. The anxiety was enough to send my mind to the bar and order five shots. I had to tell Rob I was leaving. It was a storm I could not stop.

Truth be told, when I stepped out for Christ, I was not fully prepared. I had no idea it would mean leaving the people who had watched me make the jump. I had moved dozens of times back when I was running around Born Again Lazy. I cared very little about the people—moving was part of the program. Besides, you could always make a call. Each move in the past was about my plans. I held the key to the future, and I made my own bed.

This was different. This was not about me. This was the Lord, and he wasn't taking a poll gauging my interest; he was moving me. Since the porn show, my prayers were hot with thoughts about those dying to the sin of sexual immorality. My study in the Word always seemed to wrap itself around the issues of sexual sin. I didn't ask for it. In fact, I ignored it a couple of times. I had never had a porn problem—I had always thought porn was kind of stupid. But I knew I had a voice for these people. It seemed insane. *Lord! Come on! What's going on here?*

I was being pulled into full-time ministry with XXXchurch, and I had to tell Rob, "I'm out. I'm leaving Gate Creative." I felt like a complete idiot.

To end the wondering, Craig called one day in February 2006 and let the bomb drop: He was moving to Grand Rapids, and … he wanted me to come run XXXchurch.

I was the one who had decided I was willing to do "anything short of sin," and God was pushing the envelope. If you put yourself out there, he will ask you to serve, and serve you will.

I turned to Rob. It was two-thirty on a Thursday afternoon. "Rob, I have something going on…. I have to talk to you." Usually, I can find words for even the most painful events in my life, but this time, you'll have to use your own imagination to end this story. Suffice it to say, Rob and I and the wives are still the best of friends, and God is a big God.

It was the hardest thing Diane and I had ever done, yet God fulfilled the desires of our hearts. It was our desire when I was sitting in the dining room that we would live for Christ, no matter what that meant—anything short of sin—and here we were, heading to Grand Rapids, Michigan.

I cry sometimes. Rob calls me a girl, but I do. I cry because God called a wretch like me, and I miss my friend Rob.

I love you, buddy.

Starving Jesus

MATTHEW
14:22–33

Immediately Jesus made the disciples get into the boat and go on ahead of him to the other side, while he dismissed the crowd. After he had dismissed them, he went up on a mountainside by himself to pray. When evening came, he was there alone, but the boat was already a considerable distance from land, buffeted by the waves because the wind was against it.

During the fourth watch of the night Jesus went out to them, walking on the lake. When the disciples saw him walking on the lake, they were terrified. "It's a ghost," they said, and cried out in fear.

But Jesus immediately said to them: "Take courage! It is I. Don't be afraid."

"Lord, if it's you," Peter replied, "tell me to come to you on the water."

"Come," he said.

Then Peter got down out of the boat, walked on the water and came toward Jesus. But when he saw the wind, he was afraid and, beginning to sink, cried out, "Lord, save me!"

Immediately Jesus reached out his hand and caught him. "You of little faith," he said, "why did you doubt?"

And when they climbed into the boat, the wind died down. Then those who were in the boat worshiped him, saying, "Truly you are the Son of God."

7.6
DONE

Setting that course for utter dependence on God means giving up everything and creating outreach that leaves people thinking. Blind faith in the hands of the hungry yields power and freedom to do anything short of sin to capture the imagination and passion of any generation on the planet. With that freedom and power comes a responsibility to keep yourself leveled and strong before God as you reach into your community in the name of Christ.

Why does outreach usually come in the form of mailers

and follow-up cards? Why are porn shows off-limits? Why do the nation's jails have more Islamic worship groups than Christian groups? Why do we only think about orphanages at Christmas? Why is it impossible for us to get off our butts and feed a hungry family or help someone out with a résumé to get a job? What happened to us? Aren't we the most generous country on the planet? Is it just easier to give at the office? If that's the case—stop giving at the office. Get outside and touch the hand of someone with needs. Do anything short of sin to accomplish this.

Simon Peter used every ounce of his faith and newfound freedom to do the outrageous, the unthinkable. He understood that Christ pushed the envelope and challenged the very reality people lived in. Simon Peter told the Lord, "Tell me to come," as he got ready to walk on water. Christ said, "Come." Imagine Peter, all jacked up to walk out of that boat. Surely he thought, *If Jesus can do it, so can I.* Peter did it; he stepped out. The seconds before he went over the edge must have been heart stopping. As the other disciples watched, they must have thought he was nuts. There he was, an ordinary guy, a fisherman, walking on the water. It must have been the greatest thing he had ever done. After all, he was the second human being ever to walk on water.

But Peter got distracted with fear. He saw the wind whip up, it got him nuts, and he lost faith and started to sink. He went from pure joy to sheer terror within seconds.

It is exactly the way I live. I go from dry to wet in the blink of an eye. Christ told him, "You of little faith, why did you doubt?" Have you ever noticed Simon Peter never gave Jesus an answer? Peter was wet, embarrassed, and ashamed that he had come face-to-face with his faith—and fear destroyed the moment. I still can't help thinking how cool Peter was for even trying it.

Is the lesson for us failure at the hands of fear or triumph at the hands of faith? Either way, Simon Peter was testing the waters. It would be interesting to know if

Peter mastered the art of walking on water as his life rolled out. It would have made for great outreaches and press coverage.

Walking on water was unthinkable, impossible, and outrageous. If the disciples didn't see it themselves that night, they would have thought Peter had lost his mind when he told the story. Still, how great it must have been for Peter to get back in the boat and say, "Did you see that?" I would have milked it for days.

Some days I think I can do it. Walk on water. When I'm on vacation, I even try it. I go down to the beach, look up in the air—because that's where God lives—and say, "Lord, tell me to come." I listen for a couple minutes, get bored with the lack of response, and I walk. And sink.

I do it because a part of me really thinks I can. I continue to do it, even with my past failures, because I believe eventually I will. It's that "Peter-spirit-of-possibility" that makes me do it. That day in the boat, Peter told the world that anything is possible with faith. I want and need to believe in the possibility of changing the world in the name of Christ.

J.R. is always going on about his history with God. He says faith is the only constant in his walk, and failure is assured, but faith makes it possible to try again another day. I see my history. I see the possibilities that Christ has for all of us. I have seen it among my friends and those I serve with at XXXchurch.com. We embroil ourselves in the outrageous and occasionally fail, but a lot of the time, we hit it out of the park. Peter led the charge when he stepped out of the boat that day. He told us if we act in faith, we can.

Imagine the press if someone walked on water. *Time, Newsweek,* CNN, FOX News Channel—they would be clamoring to talk with the guy who walked on water. It would be like a David Blaine event. People from all over the world would show up to watch this guy, and when he was done walking on water, they would want to touch him, talk to him, follow him, and hang on every word he said. They would worship him. Hmmm.

The church seems to overlook the value of a Walk on Water Weekend or a Friday Night Water-into-Wine Mixer. We are quick to classify outreach as sin if it looks like the world had anything to do with it. What we don't get is the extraordinary resource we have at our fingertips: the Bible. The Word should be our excuse to get rowdy in the sight of the world. We should roll out "Sinners' Dinners" and "Fasting Fridays." Our outreach needs to be outrageous. The rule should be (say it with me!) anything short of sin.

Christ didn't walk into Jerusalem—he fulfilled prophecy by riding in on a donkey. It was outrageous. He wasn't born in a nice home with all kinds of assurances he would be okay—he was born in a barn, with a feeding trough for a crib. It was outrageous. John the Baptist baptized the Son of God. Outrageous. Jesus raised people from the dead. Called the religious authority of the day "sons of the Devil." Told people he was God. Outrageous, outrageous, outrageous.

Why does God use the outrageous? Because he needs your attention. And why, when using the outrageous, does he use guys like Simon Peter? Peter was the same guy who rebuked Jesus openly, cut off a guy's ear, and denied Christ three times. I mean, come on! And with all that, Christ *still* told Peter, "On this rock I will build my church" (Matt. 16:18). Does any of this make sense?

Somewhere along the way, we've lost the ability to act outrageously in the name of Christ. If we decided to do a Walk on Water Outreach on Lake Erie, the first people to complain would be Christians. We are very willing to drive outreach from the backseat, but when the hands must get dirty, when the rubber hits the road, we have no opinion and nothing to say.

The church has lost its outrageous edge. Period. Outrageous acts of faith are not in our best interest anymore, because they require us to talk to other human beings, and communicating with people might mean that our precious comfort zone gets breached. Today, outreach is safe, with nicely contained events controlled by the politically correct. We have become a church chained to itself.

What if you decided to call sin out? What if tomorrow you got up and decided to help? Anyone? What if you decided to hold a rally to end homelessness? What if you decided to shut down orphanages? What if you stopped the new building campaign in favor of a new widow campaign or a hooker ministry? What if you just shut your mouth, got up, chucked this book in the trash, and did something, anything short of sin, to end someone's pain and misery?

JOHN 4:39-42 *Many of the Samaritans from that town believed in him because of the woman's testimony, "He told me everything I ever did." So when the Samaritans came to him, they urged him to stay with them, and he stayed two days. And because of his words many more became believers.*

They said to the woman, "We no longer believe just because of what you said; now we have heard for ourselves, and we know that this man really is the Savior of the world."

7.7 For two days, Jesus hung out with the Samaritans. It's
I NEED A DRINK funny—Jesus sent someone ahead of him to do a little outreach. A woman. Not just any woman, but a woman rife with troubles. A woman who had five husbands and who at present was "dealing" with a man who was not her husband. Christ knew she would stir it up. She's still stirring it up. She talked with Jesus for a few minutes, and he hit her hard with the truth. She believed, ran back to her village, and spread the good news.

Jesus must have been a riot to hang with. He knew this woman would rip it up for years to come. This one piece of Scripture has kept scholars busy for generations. Ask Paula White and Joyce Meyer what they think, then place a call to the pope. Jesus gave the church something to talk about and the world something to have hope in.

The woman at the well was outreach. Great outreach. Christ knew she would garner attention if she went back to town and proclaimed the arrival of the Messiah. Don't forget—many people believed as a result of her testimony, which means she was convincing. The woman did anything short of sin to get the word across. Jesus? He showed up to solidify the deal. Jesus used an outrageous, off-the-map situation to move his message throughout the world. He grabbed the attention getters, took advantage of stereotypes, and launched radical outreach to shine his light into the world. Then he turned to us and said, "Now you do it."

What a huge responsibility it is to go and make disciples. Do you ever think about that? The stats are clear: People die every day. Barna can verify. Let's not lose people without giving it our best shot. It seems we might be lost within the meetings and strategy groups; it feels as if we're dead in the water without someone's permission. We yell and scream about the next great leader when all Christ needs is someone to stand up and say, "Yeah, I'll follow."

J.R. left his career, Peter got really wet, and the woman at the well broke the gender gap. All three did anything short of sin to follow Christ. What about you?

CHAPTER

GIVE. PRAY. FAST.

8

CH 8 | GIVE. PRAY. FAST.

Do not be deceived: God cannot be mocked. A man
reaps what he sows. The one who sows to please his
sinful nature, from that nature will reap destruction;
the one who sows to please the Spirit, from the
Spirit will reap eternal life. Let us not become weary
in doing good, for at the proper time we will reap a
harvest if we do not give up. Therefore, as we have
opportunity, let us do good to all people, especially
to those who belong to the family of believers.

GALATIANS
6:7-10

When J.R and I started conceptualizing *Starving Jesus*, we
looked very hard at each other. What were our motives?
What were we trying to say? What was God trying to say?
We understand our rhetoric is not without its critics, and
rightly so. We understand that the church will never be in
a state of earthly perfection. We know the body of Christ
is big, diverse, and as such, has a million and one personality possibilities.

8.1
STARVING
JESUS?

Starving Jesus is our attempt at challenging your actions
in faith. We know salvation is not found in works, but we
understand the work involved to inspire people to the cross.
This chapter encourages you to look hard at your day-to-
day. Look hard at the physicality of your relationship with
Christ. Are you getting it done with God? Are you giving
your time, your money, and your life? Are you praying? Do
you pray with your spouse, your significant other, your
friends, and/or family? Do you pray for others? Do you understand prayer as being a necessity in your life? Have you
ever fasted food, TV, radio, video games, or whatever you
find more interesting than God? Are you starving Jesus?

Remember this: Whoever sows sparingly will also
reap sparingly, and whoever sows generously will
also reap generously. Each man should give what he

2 CORINTHIANS
9:6-8

has decided in his heart to give, not reluctantly or
under compulsion, for God loves a cheerful giver.
And God is able to make all grace abound to you, so
that in all things at all times, having all that you
need, you will abound in every good work.

8.2
GETTING IT
DONE

The body of Christ needs a giant defibrillator. We need to get two paddles the size of Jersey to lay across her chest, crank up the juice to fifty billion kagillawatts, and shock the self-righteous garbage out of her. We are so terrified by our own sin, we have ceased doing anything, and if nothing is a measure of our success, we are right on track.

Our lack of action in people's lives has led to out-of-control sin problems in every corner of our country. Recovery groups are full of people who have never met the Savior, and churches are filled with people who don't think that's a problem. We have more *justification* for sin than *actual* sin. The church went horizontal in the public arena, and the crowd is devouring its corpse. Hard to take, but true. J.R. and I are prepared for the criticism and hate mail. What we are not prepared for is more of the same.

For the record, lest we lead you astray, not everyone has his or her head inserted in the biblical sand. Our little sub-culture does have hundreds of groups and ministries that are doing some amazing things in the name of Christ, from Compassion International to a new and exciting group called Mission Year.

J.R. and I felt a responsibility to inspire people up and out of their lives in the name of Christ. We don't care if you pray for people or start a homeless shelter—we want you to act out your faith through your talents and skills for others. If you are having a hard time finding a place to connect with, we have done some of the work for you. Through this book and our Web site, www.starvingjesus.com, we have compiled a network of groups and ministries that need you. On our Web site, you will find lists of cities and organizations that are serving Christ and community. We encourage you to go, find your city, and act out your faith. We encourage you to give, fast, pray.

Be careful not to do your "acts of righteousness"   MATTHEW 6:1-4
before men, to be seen by them. If you do, you will
have no reward from your Father in heaven.
    So when you give to the needy, do not announce
it with trumpets, as the hypocrites do in the syna-
gogues and on the streets, to be honored by men. I
tell you the truth, they have received their reward in
full. But when you give to the needy, do not let your
left hand know what your right hand is doing, so
that your giving may be in secret. Then your Father,
who sees what is done in secret, will reward you.

Jesus keeps on track with one very important concept   8.3
when it comes to giving, praying, and fasting. He continu-   GIVE
ally lets us know no one needs to see what we are up to.

    To whom do you give and how much? "Anyone" and "10 percent" are usually good answers. The giver enamors us. We love hearing stories about big givers. Donald Trump lore always fills our imagination. Like the urban legend about the guy who helped The Donald change a flat tire on Trump's limo, only to get his mortgage paid off a couple days later. Givers spark our curiosity and just make us feel good. We're always saying, "If I had a million bucks, I'd help people."

    The body of Christ is skilled at writing checks and dropping a twenty in the joy box. We have amazing church buildings all over the country, from massive cathedrals to mall-like evangelical structures. It's great to be blessed with such great spaces. The money is seeing the light of day. It's the *time* we are missing in the giving equation.

    In Matthew 6, Jesus is assuming a lot about you and me, notably that we will do what he is asking. It's blind faith from the Lord. He is saying things like "When you give" and "but when you give to the needy." He starts Matthew 6 with letting you know giving will be in the form of righteous acts.

Acts have physicality to them. In other words, we will be doing something someone can see or hear or smell or feel. What are you doing?

J.R. and I are convinced the biggest thing the church is missing is physical touch. The ability to get up and just walk out of the big buildings and touch someone. I know a pastor's wife who is very honest about admitting she does not know an unsaved person. You hear her talk about it, and you get bummed out. What she's saying is "I don't have the time for the lost." Yes, the pressure on pastors' wives is enormous, but the point still stands: We have become so busy on the inside that we have forgotten about the community and their unbelief.

Giving should equal relationships. We should be striving to build new friendships and new communities every day. We should be looking constantly for ways to inject our newfound freedom into the lives of those lost and looking for Christ. Giving is not about the church, it's about the faith Christ has in us to give. He sat on a hill two thousand years ago and assumed we would.

**8.4
LET ME SHOW
YOU
SOMETHING**

It's a daunting drive over to Near West Side of Chicago if you're a visitor and a white guy who doesn't get out much. Craig and I had a nine-o'clock-in-the-morning meet and greet with our new friends from Mission Year, and we honestly didn't know what we were getting into. We've been to porn shows, but never to the 'hood.

As we exited the highway and got a little deeper into the Near West Side, it was apparent the neighborhood had seen better days. Yet it was obvious people were working hard to raise this phoenix out of the ashes.

In Chi-town, Mission Year is located in the heart of the Near West Side—an appropriate place for a ministry dedicated to putting faith into action in inner-city neighborhoods across the nation, providing a powerful combination of community service and Christian love. They tutor, build, nurture, repair, encourage, assist, organize, teach, learn from, listen to, and pray with all kinds of people, all in the name of Jesus. Mission Year wants eighteen- to twenty-nine-year-olds willing to give up one year of their lives to come and serve in one of four cities in America.

Our tour guide for the morning was a guy named Shawn who helps with recruitment for Mission Year. As you step into the Mission Year offices, located in a rehabbed, four-story brick building, you notice one thing right off the bat: These young men and women are focused. A focus that only comes from the realization that it is possible to change the world in the name of Christ. Shawn had it. Not cocky but confident in his history with a Lord and Savior who changes people forever.

Here's the undertaking of Mission Year: They want college-age kids to give up a *year.* Not a weekend or a summer ... 365 days. After these kids say "cool," they are asked not to get into any relationships or have a TV. No TV? Preposterous! Mission Year is dedicated to getting it done. Their motto says it all: "Love God. Love people. Nothing else matters."

Think about the next year of your life. Think about what you have planned and where you will go. Who will you talk to and what will you learn? Will you build? Teach? Help? Will you set the hearts and minds around you on fire for Christ?

It would be easy to start thinking Mission Year is a young man's game. It would be easy to say, "It's not for everyone," or "I don't have the time to give," or "I have this or that to do." It would be easy to walk away. The problem? The ministry of Mission Year serves as a living example for you and me; it is faith in action.

Halfway through our meet and greet, Shawn said, "Let me take you into a community where we're living and making a difference in the lives of people." Craig and I had no idea what it was going to look like. We had our assumptions about city outreach: It's feeding people, it's getting people money, it's clothing people. We were blind to what was happening on the Near West Side of Chicago. Sometimes we are so exclusive, we miss seeing ministry like Mission Year.

Shawn drove us through crack-infested neighborhoods, where flashing blue lights on telephone poles indicate gunfire. It was no porn show, and it certainly was not the neighborhood to get lost in. Shawn pulled around the corner and parked on a busy main street. Craig and I got a little nervous. Being men of pride, we acted as if we do this all the time.

This block was different from the others. It was clean, and the people standing outside the buildings were smiling and laughing. We—three white guys with big grins and mall clothes—were standing in the middle of the Lawndale community. We were looking at years of faith in action that had been created with the community in mind. Here was a busy urban area thriving with community outreach. Halfway houses, restaurants, health clinics, beauty shops, a church, computer training facilities, and construction just starting on a new music school—this was truly amazing.

Shawn went on to tell us that one church several years ago did all of it. They bought building after building, so the community could be better, stronger, and able to serve one another. And years later it's still happening. The health clinic across the street is state of the art and brimming with people out to do one thing—help each other.

At one end of the block, Shawn led us into the Hope Palace, a halfway house designed to help men just out of prison. I met a twenty-three-year-old man named Cheo, who said, "This place is my next start." I could see Shawn looking at Craig and me. He was hoping we were getting it, getting what he saw the first time he came down here.

The first time Shawn came to this street, he was filled with the idea of helping and serving this community through Mission Year. His preconceived notions about ministry ran cross-grain to the reality of this place that was filled with immediate needs. Needs that a quick prayer or a quick meal or ten bucks couldn't necessarily solve. This place had issues, and understanding that meant abandoning everything he knew.

For months, he and his wife struggled to fit in. Imagine you're newly married, white, on fire for the Lord; and you move into a predominantly black community, hoping to serve. Shawn and his wife didn't know what they were doing, but they knew they were doing something, anything short of sin, and that was enough.

They had a heck of a time adjusting to their new life. Finding friends. Finding their way around. Understanding the car will get broken into from time to time and their skin color could be problematic. This was what following the Lord looked like for Shawn and his new bride. For months, they thought they might have made a mistake, until they realized God just needs you to show up and give of your time. He doesn't need the future to be paved with perfect plans—he needs your time and availability.

Shawn had promised himself he would take a lesser seat as he moved into the Lawndale community, afraid of becoming a personality at the expense of the ministry. He was content to sideline himself. He was missing opportunities because he didn't get that the tools he needed to use for outreach were the very gifts and talents God had already given him.

Shawn is a drummer—a very good drummer. About six months into working with Mission Year, he and his wife made a decision. "We would give it six more months, and if it wasn't happening by that time, we were going to pack it up," he said. After making their decision, Shawn met a guy who played in a church band in Lawndale. Shawn mentioned he played drums, and the gentleman invited him to band practice.

Shawn walked into band practice with no expectation other than meeting new people and going where he thought the Lord was directing. After the awkward greetings and questions about what he was doing there, the band started practice. Shawn sat in the back, content in the lesser seat. At the end of practice he was invited up to play. Again, Shawn was leery about letting it rip; he didn't want a spotlight; he just wanted to serve. He sat behind that drum kit, looked around, and started playing. "I felt like I'd been waiting for that my entire life," he said. Needless to say, Shawn ripped it up and was invited to play with the band.

That practice became the door Shawn and his wife walked through. It served as a reminder: Service is not necessarily biblical dissertations or the ability to understand apologetics or to serve food at a shelter. It may not be Africa or Haiti—it may just be showing up at a band practice. Shawn took the lesser seat, and as a result, God placed his talent in the community for everyone. Shawn just needed to show up.

There wasn't a person on that street who didn't know Shawn as we walked around. He went into the shelter, the clinic, the church; and everyone smiled and hugged him, proud and happy to see him. Shawn is changing the world. He is showing up, giving his time, giving his life. This wasn't about black or white, rich or poor—this is about a guy and his wife throwing down for a community and just making up their minds that this is where they will live and love. They are giving.

Later that day, Craig and I were excited. Shawn's face had said it all. This was a guy who had found peace and contentment living out his faith. We were quiet on the way back to the hotel. Sometimes giving will speak so loudly it literally quiets you. When you find silence that powerful, you should listen.

We are inherently drawn to giving. The Bible coupled this with an inherent desire to serve. God is the voice that drives us. When you give, be prepared for change. Be prepared to lose sight of your goals and dreams for someone else's favor. Christ gave his life for you and me, and when we acknowledge that, the Holy Spirit drives us to give. It will become the air we breathe.

Mission Year was created with that very desire to be played out on city streets. Your desire can play out anywhere. You don't need permission, you don't need money—you only need the courage to lay yourself down and give.

Then little children were brought to Jesus for him to place his hands on them and pray for them. But the disciples rebuked those who brought them.

Jesus said, "Let the little children come to me, and do not hinder them, for the kingdom of heaven belongs to such as these." When he had placed his hands on them, he went on from there.

MATTHEW 19:13-15

Jesus was all too happy to pray for the kids. He loved them. Even said the kingdom belongs to them. Jesus understood the hope and sense of wonder kids bring to the table. He understood kids to be honest and open as they question the world around them.

8.5
EASY

Do you have a kid in your life? Maybe your own? Maybe you know the neighbor's kid, or you have a niece or nephew. What's your direct influence in a kid's life? What do kids see when they look at you? Are you living a life a kid can emulate or approve of?

J.R. and I set a few goals for *Starving Jesus*, one of which we saw as the most glaring immediate need in the world today: kids. From food to families, kids are getting the short end of the stick through no fault of their own. Christ calls us directly to deal with the immediate needs of kids.

Tonight before you crawl into bed, after you've watched some TV and had a great meal, here's a great prayer you can take to God. Ask God how you can help the 500,000-plus American kids in foster care or the millions of kids who are going to bed without food or families. Guilty yet? Us too.

Here we are, the light to the world, and we aren't even close to eradicating child hunger anywhere. In the county where we are writing this book, there are 150 kids available today for adoption and 60 kids under the age of eighteen sitting in juvenile detention. Not to mention the hundred or so kids floating in and out of foster care. I don't care what the arguments are about these kids. I don't care if they are troubled, physically disabled, mentally challenged, drug addicted, violent. What I do care about is our response; we've got to snatch these kids up in the name of Christ.

Fifty years ago, evangelist Everett Swanson was challenged by a missionary friend to do something. In 1952 Everett was traveling in South Korea when he was confronted with the immediate needs of children who were displaced by war. His missionary friend simply said, "What do you intend to do about this?" Not, "Don't worry. God will do something." The friend understood immediate need, and that meant people giving time and money to get down and dirty to help these kids, because the kids weren't capable of helping themselves.

Reverend Swanson headed back to the States, and upon his arrival, he received cash—cold hard cash—to support the kids. That was enough for Everett to get it. The good reverend stepped forward in faith, acted out his belief, and today you and I know his organization by the name of Compassion International. Compassion provides child development aid to more than 728,800 children in more than twenty countries. For us, the greatest part of the story is the issuing challenge to Swanson and then the following action that set into motion one of the greatest worldwide outreaches to date.

He had one challenge: give. He stepped up and gave. It was a great act of faith. What about you? Some would like this book to be all nice and positive with flowery speech and room to take nice little positive notes. Here's the deal. When you signed up with Christ, he changed your life. He then asked you to lose your life and follow him. If you need help understanding what that call looks like, take a peek at Everett Swanson. He didn't sit around thinking about doing—he did. His life was service to God and God's people. I can guarantee you it was hard work. The best thing you can do for the kids of the world is to give your time and money. Compassion has made it easy. Completely transparent and filled with the love of Christ, this organization is only getting better. Hit the site at www.starvingjesus.com/compassion to sponsor a child today. It will cost you about thirty-two bucks a month, but you will change the life of one child forever. One of the goals of *Starving Jesus* is to see five hundred children get sponsored. Stop the excuses, stretch yourself in faith, and let the kids of the world see Christ with your giving.

And when you pray, do not be like the hypocrites, MATTHEW
for they love to pray standing in the synagogues and 6:5-15
on the street corners to be seen by men. I tell you
the truth, they have received their reward in full. But
when you pray, go into your room, close the door
and pray to your Father, who is unseen. Then your
Father, who sees what is done in secret, will reward
you. And when you pray, do not keep on babbling
like pagans, for they think they will be heard be-
cause of their many words. Do not be like them, for
your Father knows what you need before you ask
him.

This, then, is how you should pray:
    "Our Father in heaven,
    hallowed be your name,
    your kingdom come,
    your will be done
    on earth as it is in heaven.

> Give us today our daily bread.
> Forgive us our debts,
> as we also have forgiven our debtors.
> And lead us not into temptation,
> but deliver us from the evil one."
> For if you forgive men when they sin against you,
> your heavenly Father will also forgive you. But if you
> do not forgive men their sins,
> your Father will not forgive your sins.

8.6 PRAY

My preteen niece, Rachel, is what I call a common-wisdom freak. She is able to dish out spiritually discerning wisdom. It blows my mind, a kid with enough discernment to fill the seats at Willow Creek.

If you are lucky enough to engage this young lady in conversation, it can be awesomely horrible as you are reminded that the wisdom of God has very little to do with education or even life experience. Sometimes it comes in the form of a young girl.

Rachel is my sister-in-law's kid. A couple times a year her family comes to visit. All six of them. Paul and Karen, Rachel's mom and dad, are great friends, and we always have a great time together. The kids bring a spark and an energy to the house that only kids can, coupled with my lessons about the origins of words like "booger" and "fart." It's a riot!

Visiting Uncle J.R. and Aunt Diane is a big deal for the kids. Diane and I are always aware of what that means to each kid. We make time for everyone. We want so much to speak into their lives about Christ and his freedom. Rachel is a voracious reader, and I guarantee you she has read more books than I have. She inspires me to read, and although I probably won't read more than I already do, it's always good to be inspired. She has read the Bible cover to cover a few times and has even memorized chunks of the Word. Again, inspiration.

Rachel watches Di and me very closely. She sees the way we talk about others and the way we live out our faith. A few years ago, they were visiting, and we decided to take a trip to the mall. Rachel's dad, Paul, used to drive this outrageously large travel van. It was like a bus. We all piled into the van, and off we went.

Rachel and I were in the middle seats in the back of the van with perfect window views, and we were making everyone laugh with play-by-play commentary of what was going on in the cars traveling next to us. One guy had an ugly dog in the backseat, one old lady had a giant hat, and one girl driving next to us was smoking.

"Ahhh!" I said. "Look at that girl smoking! That's disgusting, and she's so young! What's the deal with that?"

Diane chimed in. "Yeah, don't ever do that."

Without skipping a beat, Rachel said, "I pray for smokers."

"What?" I said, very interested.

"Every time I see a smoker, I pray for them."

"What's the prayer?"

"I ask God to help them stop smoking, and if they don't know Jesus, that they soon would."

She said it so confidently and so full of trust, it freaked me out. I looked around the van for God. Her faith was unshakable, her eyes fixed on mine. Rachel needed me to know that not only did she pray for these people, but she also knew God was going to help them because of that prayer. I was stunned. This little prepubescent girl took a hammer and dented my reality to the point of speechlessness.

I certainly wasn't praying for people like that. The most I could muster was, "Please help this guy or that gal for this or that." I wasn't fixed and focused on God really doing something. I was merely placating God with the sound of my voice.

Rachel had disrupted something in me. The idea that prayer is more than just petition—prayer is to be the very fabric of how I walk each day. Prayer has to be in front of everything I do and everywhere I go. Prayer is my relationship with God and with the work around me. And here a twelve-year-old was giving a very good lesson about prayer ... and faith. I felt as if I should be learning from her.

Rachel believed and was filled with hope. Hope for what is and what will be. She was sitting in a van, changing the lives of those around her. It was powerful and humbling. I don't *know* if that young girl stopped smoking, but I'm willing to *bet* she's smoke free.

Christ knew we would struggle with prayer. He knew praying to a God we can't see or touch would be problematic. That's why he taught us exactly how to pray. That's why he challenged the disciples to pray. Jesus would go off for hours—sometimes all night—and pray. He did this consistently, so you and I would know the value of prayer, the value of talking with the Father alone about whatever. Rachel got it. She knew faith acted itself out in prayer. She knew it wasn't about batting 1.000. It was simply asking God to do whatever it is we cannot or sometimes just don't want to do.

MARK 11:22-25   *"Have faith in God," Jesus answered. "I tell you the truth, if anyone says to this mountain, 'Go, throw yourself into the sea,' and does not doubt in his heart but believes that what he says will happen, it will be done for him. Therefore I tell you, whatever you ask for in prayer, believe that you have received it, and it will be yours. And when you stand praying, if you hold anything against anyone, forgive him, so that your Father in heaven may forgive you your sins."*

We got to the mall, and I started looking. Looking to change people's lives with prayer. I was praying for everyone. It fit like a glove; it was as natural as breathing.

Prayer is one those pesky things Christians fall in and out of without much conversation. We take it for granted—somehow it's always there—yet we do a great job ignoring the act. Give yourself a routine with prayer. Earlier in the book we prescribed twice a day, morning and night. Do the two until you build regularity with prayer. Once you can count on it, your faith will naturally start acting itself out with prayer.

From time to time when I see Rachel, I remind her about that day. She just smiles, unaware of the impact she had in my life. Unaware, I'm sure, of the many lives she has and will change with prayer.

When you fast, do not look somber as the hypocrites do, for they disfigure their faces to show men they are fasting. I tell you the truth, they have received their reward in full. But when you fast, put oil on your head and wash your face, so that it will not be obvious to men that you are fasting, but only to your Father, who is unseen; and your Father, who sees what is done in secret, will reward you.

MATTHEW 6:16-18

The body of Christ does not fast. We are very comfortable with food in this country. From the miles and miles of restaurant strip malls to our obsession with anything fast food, we have become fast-less. And those who do fast? Freaks.

8.7 FAST

The world has done a great job at making fasting "unhealthy" and irrelevant to our lives. For the most part, the church has joined these voices. The Christian mind-set is that fasting should be something you're called to do.

That is simply not the truth. Jesus uses a word that indicates you will fast. He says, "*When* you fast." Not, "If you think about it next week," or "Maybe if you get around to it." Christ calls every follower to fast—everyone. You can stop sitting on the fence from here on out. If you crave a deeper relationship with God, you will fast. There are no rules for fasting other than watching your motives about fasting. Translation: Do not wear fasting like a badge of courage or honor. Christ is very clear about this in Matthew 6.

As I said earlier, my first forty-day fast changed my life. Next to marrying my wife, Diane, it was the best experience

8.8 FORTY DAYS

of my life, hands down. Why? It drove me closer to God at an exhilarating pace. It was an immediate connection with the Maker of the universe. It divorced me from me, so I would become solely dependent on the Lord. It gave me insight to God that I never would have had if I hadn't fasted. It solidified my faith in him. I said one sentence over and over again during my forty days: "He is real!" I was surprised every time I said it. Fasting healed relationships around me. It touched the lives of people around me.

People ask me all the time, "Do I have to fast for forty days?" I answer this way: "I felt a strong attachment to forty days, given Christ's fast. His fast was inspired through the Spirit, and as such he did what the Spirit led him to do."

MATTHEW 4:1-3   *Then Jesus was led by the Spirit into the desert to be tempted by the devil. After fasting forty days and forty nights, he was hungry. The tempter came to him and said, "If you are the Son of God, tell these stones to become bread."*

Jesus had a mission of sorts. Being led into the wilderness by the Spirit had its implications at the time. Jesus knew he would face the Devil, and the fast prepared him to do so. A forty-day fast should be entered into with prodding from the Holy Spirit. It is a long and arduous commitment, one that will remove you from the world, testing your faith and every fiber of your being. It will bring you great joy and great pain, but it will change your life.

The not-eating thing does mess with your mind. You become so hungry at times you are willing to eat the couch, or you will watch your dog eat and get mad. Eventually you fall into a rhythm when you fast for long or short periods of time. The rhythm will encompass great amounts of time in prayer and study in the Word. Make no mistake—you will be hungry. At times you will be miserable, you will yell at your spouse, get angry with the kids. You will doubt, you will count the days—but you will love it.

Don't worry about the numbers. Whether it's one meal or six weeks, the act of fasting, regardless of the time commitment, is enough for you to start building a stronger walk with Christ.

In the church at Antioch there were prophets and teachers: Barnabas, Simeon called Niger, Lucius of Cyrene, Manaen (who had been brought up with Herod the tetrarch) and Saul. While they were worshiping the Lord and fasting, the Holy Spirit said, "Set apart for me Barnabas and Saul for the work to which I have called them." So after they had fasted and prayed, they placed their hands on them and sent them off.

ACTS 13:1-3

Scenario after scenario, the Bible is filled with people who have incredible needs that drive them to lay their bodies down before the Lord in the form of a fast. The church doesn't know what to say about the physicality of a fast. Some churches fall away from the long fast, claiming it's just not healthy. Others suggest anything but a food fast. Our tendency is to listen to the doctors and health experts of the world. It's an easy trap.

8.9
NECESSITY

The first thing to understand about the physicality of a fast is that God the Father will be your food in the form of prayer and his Word. Yes, there are some commonsense things about fasting when it comes to your health; let the Holy Spirit guide you. Most people will ask, "Can I drink juice?" "Can I drink smoothies?" "Can I have a protein supplements?" Yes, to all of those things, providing you are praying and using the discernment of the Holy Spirit as you enter the fast.

When I fast, I drink water and juice. That's it. I have done enough fasting that I understand how my body will react, and let me tell you, your body will be the last thing you are concerned with as you build fasting into your life. Remember, God has you. Try not to draw the fast away from God by worrying about your body. Your body will go through dramatic changes. You will lose weight; that's a nice thing for those of us who are heavier than we should be. You will be afraid to fart; I'll let you learn about that yourself. You will reach states of euphoria, and you will want to cut your head off. Bottom line: Place your faith in Christ. Fasting will change your life.

Prayer and study take on necessity as you roll out your fast. You will be drawn to your knees. You will dig into the Bible. Sometimes you won't know what you're looking for, but you will go to the Word searching for him. In prayer, God will touch you with peace so incredibly out of this world that you will never want to leave its comfort. The Bible will cease to be a book and will become the very breath of God. Am I being dramatic? No.

When it's all said and done and time to eat, you will mourn the loss of its experience and miss the comfort of its view. You will inevitably go back. If you are not a fasting Christian, it's time you get off your derriere and starve a little for the Lord. It is a great opportunity to strengthen your walk, as well as impact lives around you.

CH 9 | THE ACT OF ACTING

May the Lord show mercy to the household of One-
siphorus, because he often refreshed me and was
not ashamed of my chains.

2 TIMOTHY 1:16

When J.R. conceived the whole Starving Jesus thing, I was more than happy to entertain his ramblings about fasting and the American church's ability to ignore God.

9.1
2:07 A.M.

After his first fast, he was obsessed about the Starving Jesus concept. Nonstop every day, all the time. If you know him, you know you can't shut him off until something happens, and that something was more than I think we bargained for.

We travel a lot together, keeping each other account-able and company, frankly. The road is hard and lonely. Away from family and friends. We always manage to have a great time and, on occasion, get into some good trouble. I'm not talking people being mad at us; I'm talking about the ideas we dream up as we head back to the hotel after an event. It's funny—we don't need pens or paper. We just talk and the craziest things pop out.

In March 2006 we were in Boston, doing a porn debate with legendary porn star Ron Jeremy. Ron, for those of you keeping yourselves away from pop culture, is considered the most iconic porn star on the planet, having personally starred in 1,800-plus porn films since the '70s. I debate Ron regularly on college campuses across the country. It's nuts—me, porn pastor, and Ron, porn king, debating. The students eat it up, and XXXchurch gets a good shot at shooting a message to a generation that so desperately needs to hear it: Porn sucks. J.R. laughs, because most of the time I am booed and Ron gets standing ovations.

It turns out that Ron is a great guy, in need of a whole lot of love. It breaks our hearts. As of this writing he doesn't know Christ. If the debates ever stop, you'll know some-thing great happened.

Starving Jesus

In March there we were in Boston, freezing our butts off, walking back to the hotel with Ron Jeremy! Sometimes I get these bird's-eye views of our lives and think, *What are we doing?* We get in the lobby, Ron is hungry—nothing out of the ordinary here, Ron likes to eat. We head to the hotel bar and eat and talk for four hours. Four hours! Turns out porn stars can talk, a lot.

J.R. and I indulge every single question Ron has about God, hell, and the virgin birth. We're not great theologians, but we can hold our own. The bar of the hotel turned into church; it was a great opportunity to love a guy who just needed companionship without strings attached, and we were all about telling him how Christ had changed our lives. Guess what? He listened.

Needless to say, as the conversation wound down, we were hopped up. J.R. was bouncing as if he just got a crack fix, and I was truly grateful to have had the chance to love Ron Jeremy and show him Christ.

We got back to the room and literally went over everything we'd said, looking for any possible translation in Ron's words that might indicate he's ready to jump ship and take up the cross. We were thrilled, happy, ready to take on the world. I don't know, but I do know that all the rhetoric that J.R. had been spewing started to come to the top as we both realized that Starving Jesus meant jumping on these types of opportunities and biting down, hard. After all, we are the church when church isn't around.

Ron has big needs, needs like you and me. He needs Christ, and for four hours we put it all out: every word, every sentence, every breath we had. Not caring about his fame or whether this guy likes us or what the others heard in the bar or hoping we'd have a relationship with him after dinner. We listened to the call of the Holy Spirit and dove in with both feet, and by the time we got back to the room, Starving Jesus had been kick-started and was racing in full gear. God had inspired us through a porn star. That's a ludicrous sentence, but it's how God works.

We had come to that point: Crap or get off the pot, play ball or go home. We both knew, staring at each other, it was time to act on Starving Jesus. Stop talking about it, dreaming about it, thinking about it, praying about it, and just freaking do something.

I have much to write to you, but I do not want to use paper and ink. Instead, I hope to visit you and talk with you face to face, so that our joy may be complete.

2 JOHN 12

In my best moments, I am still a vile little redhead, desperate for attention and the approval of those around me. I am always on the lookout for opportunities for me, situations that will glorify me. It's the way it is, and I suppose I will be chasing the Lord on these issues for the rest of my life.

9.2
40 DAYS OF NOTHING

Part of me says, "Don't work so hard at change." Another part of me sees a hotel bar in Boston as the chance to lie completely down and get it done, because some guy in the past did the same for me. In those moments I drive toward selflessness, and the world makes the most sense. I am at peace, knowing my purpose as God gives me the words and wisdom to help change another guy's life.

After meeting Ron in Boston, the hotel room was buzzing with possibilities. Craig and I were anxious about having the Starving Jesus conversation. It was finally moving from ramped-up, crazy rhetoric to physically doing something. Letting people know it's okay to stand up and take one for the team, because we're supposed to. Simple, right?

We knew we had to write the message of *Starving Jesus*, but a publisher would want time lines, meetings, and phone calls. We needed to spit this at the world—now. There would be no waiting for anyone, only us acting because that's what we do. No permission needed, only two guys with something to say about faith in relationship to everyone around us. We were ready to literally carve *Starving Jesus* in the wood of Christian subculture.

We made the first *SJ* decision right there in that hotel room. Write the book and publish it with or without a publisher. A big risk, because it meant cash for the project was coming out of our pockets. Books are not cheap to publish.

Past the book-writing dilemma, the ideas were flying all over the room. From a Starving Jesus billboard campaign all over the country to the one idea we locked on to. "Why don't we chain ourselves to a church for forty days?" I said, thinking it might be a little over the top.

Gross looked at me inquisitively. "Where?" he asked, as if he was actually considering this.

"Let's find the biggest church in the country, let's go, not say a thing, chain ourselves up for forty days ... if we get arrested, so what." As it was coming out of my mouth, I was having one of those Gross bird's-eye-view moments, and I was saying, "What am I doing?"

Craig loved it but modified it a little: "How about we go from LA to New York in forty days, chaining ourselves to churches as we go?"

I quickly added without thinking, "Yeah, and we'll fast too!" The room got quiet for a minute or two as we rolled it around in our heads. "This is gonna piss everyone off or move a lot people. They're either gonna love it or hate it," I said less confidently than I had been a few seconds earlier, realizing the possibility I could be a future ex-con.

As we talked into the morning, we created the Starving Jesus Tour. The end would justify the means as we landed on taking an RV from coast to coast in forty days. We agreed on fasting for the forty but conceded the idea of chaining ourselves to a church in lieu of chaining ourselves to a pew. We would get an old pew, drill holes through it, and chain ourselves to it anywhere we found a lot of people gathered. Churches, public places, streets, in front of the Golden Gate Bridge, the White House, the Love sign in Philly, Times Square. We thought it was brilliant. What could go wrong, right? I mean, our slogan spoke for itself: "Starving Jesus, the 40 Days of Nothing Tour." Who wouldn't love that?

Beyond the book and tour, we agreed we needed something tangible for people to embrace for the 40 Days of Nothing. We can't hit the road, speak at forty churches, and not have something for people. Just by the very nature of what we were doing we needed a "do as we do" activity based on the needs of the world and the acting out of faith.

We both love Compassion International and are always looking for ways to join forces to help such a great ministry. That night as we talked, Craig looked up at me and said, "Think we can sponsor five hundred kids in forty days?"

"Five hundred? No way!" I quickly spit back.

"Ye of little faith. I think we can do it," Craig said as he got up and paced widely. "Then we can go to the country where the kids are from and visit them, showing everyone the reality of what stepping out looks like." I had to admit it was good. Great! Every now and then Gross comes up with a gem, and that was a gem.

We landed on Compassion kids from the Dominican Republic. The DR is about an hour flying time from Miami, going east. It's a poor country, and help is needed bigtime. I felt proud of us as we laid the foundation stones for the tour. It blew me away what the Holy Spirit was giving birth to.

We tend to move quickly once the idea is out in the open. Sometimes moving quickly can lead to apologies; other times it's exactly what the doctor ordered. Most of the time we find success in moving forward quickly.

We make no apologies for our methods as we push the gospel into the world. Going forward means you are willing to take steps that the majority of those around you will not. This is what makes you a disciple, the act of acting. These ideas don't have to be big ideas; the subculture is already oversaturated with Christians who have the next big Jesus idea. Truthfully, we don't need any more ideas, just people to execute existing ideas.

This is the message of the Starving Jesus Tour: Execute your faith. For forty days, we wanted the church world to see two idiots executing an idea wrapped up in faith—not just talk, not just write a book we can whore out at the next convention or create a new five-part series to sell on the Web site. Two living, breathing dudes, putting it all out so others may be inspired to act as well.

JOHN 12:47 *As for the person who hears my words but does not keep them, I do not judge him. For I did not come to judge the world, but to save it.*

9.3
RUBBER AND
THE ROAD

If we had concerns, we certainly didn't talk about them. Immediately, I booked an RV out of San Francisco one way. Destination: New York City. Turns out RVs are expensive—especially one way. A thirty-one-foot Winnebago with one bedroom, a living room–type area, and a sitting area that doubled as a bed, plus a sink, a bathroom, even a shower—it all seemed so glamorous. Never having experienced RV living, it seemed fun, adventurous, even a bit exciting. The open road, meeting new people, freedom. That line of thinking would turn out to be crap ... just plain crap. Little did we realize forty days in an RV with no food would take a massive toll on all of our lives.

We set the engine in motion. J.R. would handle all the logistics, and I would book dates and venues. We sent an e-mail to everyone on our XXXchurch e-mail list and essentially said, "If you have a church, we want to come." We laughed as we sent it out. No way would forty churches respond, no way. Here's the e-mail announcement J.R. wrote:

On August 5, 2006, pastors, authors, and speakers Craig Gross and J.R. Mahon jump into an RV and head out on a 40-day, 40-city tour across the United States. The tour begins in northern California and concludes 40 days later in New York City on September 13. The tour is designed to help church communities effect change in their cities and inspire Christians to act out their faith.

"Get out of the pews and into people's lives," says J.R.

Craig continues, "We have a responsibility when it comes to our communities, we must get up and out ... serve in the name of Christ."

J.R. and Craig will stop at a church every day, challenging, inspiring, and helping people out of the pews and into the community. They will speak to congregations, pray, hold Starving Jesus Bible studies, and inspire new church outreach.

In every city and congregation they visit, the team will provide tangible ways to get involved in the community. They have compiled a comprehensive list of organizations in every city that need the body of Christ. The Web site, www.starvingjesus.com, will also become a clearinghouse for creative outreach within your city.

Craig and J.R. will be fasting the entire 40 days of the tour and will encourage others to pray and fast as well.

The duo will take out ads in major magazines and Web sites promoting this movement with the goal of getting at least 1,000 people to commit to praying and fasting for the tour.

Whether someone fasts one day and one city of the tour, or the whole 40 days, it's their goal to see people turn nothing into something.

THERE IS NO COST TO YOU!!!! THE ONLY THING WE NEED IS A PARKING LOT.

So ... join the Starving Jesus Tour ... this is what you get.

J.R. and Craig will:

1. Speak to your church, ministry, youth group, or college.

2. Lead a Starving Jesus Bible study.

3. Lead discussion groups about discipleship.

4. Help your church, ministry, college lead a community-wide call to faith.

5. Provide your church, ministry, college with information about Christ-centered organizations in your community needing help.

Here we come, please call or write us ...

I will admit that I am geographically challenged; I should not have been in charge of booking the locations. J.R. kept asking me if I knew what I was doing, but I was sure we wouldn't book this thing. When they called and e-mailed back, I just plugged them in regardless of where they were. If they were close to the cities we picked and could work with the dates, they were in. It was that simple.

We were amazed! By the end of the week after the e-mail went out, the Starving Jesus Tour was booked. Booked!

Forty churches, forty days. It was booked. It was odd: Either people were encouraged by the message of Starving Jesus or churches simply had nothing going on in the months of August and September.

These were his instructions: "Take nothing for the journey except a staff—no bread, no bag, no money in your belts. Wear sandals but not an extra tunic. Whenever you enter a house, stay there until you leave that town. And if any place will not welcome you or listen to you, shake the dust off your feet when you leave, as a testimony against them."

MARK 6:8-11

I was thinking as I was calling every church that had booked a tour date, *Man, this is gonna be an adventure of a lifetime. How many folks get these kinds of opportunities?* Not many, I'm sure. Part of me was in it for the fame. I was putting myself at the starting line with the wind blowing through my hair and looking out over the open road thinking we were the only dudes doing this kind of thing. *Man, aren't we great? We are modern-day apostles. Put us in the Paul Hall of Fame, write songs about us, blog about us, do what you must, because we truly deserve it!*

9.4
PROVING
OURSELVES
WRONG

I was drunk with the thought of being propped up, establishing a new conversation about church and all that it isn't and all it should be. My mind ran selfishly out of control. I was consumed by my own press and believing it. Thanking God for the voice, not understanding he would take it away, because he gave it to me. Very dangerous stuff considering I regularly rant against this type of behavior.

During the calls I quickly understood the reality of what was ahead. This was gonna be work. Not work like stuffing envelopes, but serious relationship building with folks all over the country. Each church had its own personality, and each stop was coming with its own Christian garbage about church and what needs to be done. The Starving

Jesus Tour for some churches was a way to say, "Look, congregant people! This is what I have been saying all along." I would laugh out loud as I called each ministry that joined the tour, because it became blatantly clear that the SJ tour might become an altar call for the church.

The humility started rolling in when I was on the phone with the guy who booked us in the middle of Georgia. As I was dialing the number, I was looking for the dude's name, and I thought I read it wrong. The e-mail said, "Call Ollie." Ollie? Who names their kid Ollie? I mean, come on! Does anyone know an Ollie? Umm, no.

"Hello," said a guy on the other end who sounded like an Ollie. "Hey, man, it's J.R. with Starving Jesus. You cool to talk?"

"Oh yeah!!!!!" he says with a southern accent like you'd expect every trucker to have. "Hey, J.R., man, I just want to say what you guys are doing is awesome; it will change a generation. It is changing me."

I am such an egoist all I heard was, "Man, you are great." It wasn't until I heard about his plans prior to our arrival in his little corner of the world that I finally got what the Starving Jesus Tour would mean for people.

Ollie goes on to tell me during our short conversation that the month before we arrive, he will be in Ukraine setting up a church and bringing Christ to a country that so desperately needs God. He's saying things like "I am so grateful to have a chance to do this"; "I can't believe God is having me do this"; "It's a privilege to go." On and on, he's humble as a church mouse, and on and on I am beating my head on the desk, thinking, *Who cares about forty days in an RV with two jerks bent on getting people up and out. Not only is this guy getting off his butt, he's also humble about it.* Sickening. Lesson learned: I am not the center of all things ministry. Shocker, I know.

The nutty thing—everyone I was talking to across the country gave me one very frightening thought: We might be proving ourselves wrong. What if, God forbid, the church really isn't in trouble and we just love to rant? What if the body of Christ as a whole is doing all right? What if the people in the American church *are* helping people? Man, that would suck.

I was imagining us rolling in to Times Square and seeing that the Christian subculture had posted banners that read "You Guys Are Idiots." For a minute, I was worried—until I got this e-mail from the lead pastor at the church in Texas.

> OK, guys ...
>
> I sent you a 2-page e-mail that you never responded to. I am hosting you in Texas. You ignored the ministries I asked you to highlight and have none of the pertinent information about schedule, etc., that I busted to send you on your blog. The ONLY thing I have heard from you is constant requests to know what hotel you're staying at, which is very ironic considering the supposed nature of your tour. Could we get a little more help here, please?

You gotta love Christians. I stopped worrying. We'd be fine....

A simple man believes anything,
but a prudent man gives thought to his steps.

PROVERBS
14:15

The nuts and bolts of this thing were enough to drive you nuts. From driving directions to the cast of characters, we needed to pull off a forty-day, forty-night tour across the country. Did I mention the fasting?

9.5
NUTS AND
BOLTS

We knew we needed to film the entire tour, so the search began to find a documentary guy who could survive forty days on the road. We also needed a driver. There was talk about the two of us taking turns driving. Just talk.

We found our cast of characters among the great people who surround XXXchurch.com. Our video guy, a tall, lanky documentary producer from the Pacific Northwest. The driver, Dave Belles, who affectionately became known as Dave the Driver. Dave is a forty-something ex-lacrosse jock from upstate New York.

The physicality of a forty-day tour was maddening. A lot of people, from very well-known churches to small-town congregations, e-mail XXXchurch wanting to know how we do things. We work out of basements, coffee-houses, and airports. We don't have a machine or a large staff behind the ministry. The only thing we have going for us is the impulsiveness to have an idea and act on it. Whether it means spending our money or asking for cash, we simply just go and execute.

The Starving Jesus project—from book, tour, movie, to Web site—was no different. We worried about losing our shirts on the project, but whatever. God would surely bless our efforts, provided we stuck close and didn't act like two idiots bent on some form of weird Christian fame.

The deal is easy when it comes to outreach, even if the outreach is for the church: You act. I would be rich if I had a buck for every time someone told me, "I wish we could …" or "We're thinking about it," or "I am trying." And the killer of all killers for outreach: "We are waiting on God to fund us."

God is not a bank, nor is he the planning committee. Stop the useless praying and the whiny, aggravating talk about what you're gonna do, and just act. "Oh, but my church won't let me," "Oh, but my pastor will never …" "Oh, my de-nomination will never go for that." Well, then convert. This whole Jesus thing really doesn't need you anyway.

Jesus dismissed a few folks along the way. We don't play on some happy, nice playground with faith and salvation; we don't take breaks and have snack time. Last time I checked, they beat him beyond recognition and let him die so you and I could take the message to the world, because we get it. Starving Jesus works the same way.

The tour and book couldn't be about the money, although

at times it was. It couldn't be about J.R. or me, although at times it was and is, and we have paid a price for selfish endeavoring.

We prayed this thing would change people's lives, took the risk, and went after it. We were acting out in faith. We need to stop worrying about our little corners of the world and start understanding that these acts, one after another, add up, and God honors us accordingly. But remember, it's not a give-and-get program. J.R. and I have little choice on this crazy ride; we couldn't have predicted this book or tour. God filled our hearts with our crazy rhetoric and nutty, unabridged passion, and we simply stood up and said, "Let's do it!"

How about you? What has he placed in your heart right now, this very minute? We understand the tug, the pull on your heart right this very second. What we don't get is the lack of action. Apprehension can kill a spiritual buzz. So perform some preventive maintenance on your spiritual well-being. Give, fast, and pray your way into acting out faith.

Now we pray to God that you will not do anything wrong. Not that people will see that we have stood the test but that you will do what is right even though we may seem to have failed. For we cannot do anything against the truth, but only for the truth. We are glad whenever we are weak but you are strong; and our prayer is for your perfection.

2 CORINTHIANS 13:7-9

I don't think we prayed enough for the tour. Don't get me wrong, there was praying. Our wives, us, family, friends; people prayed for safety, health, changed lives. We were straight with God. In hindsight, I wish my prayers had been centered around the team on the RV. I wish I had asked for the RV to be a holy place, that Dave the Driver and his teenage kids would be happy. I wish I had prayed that

9.6
IT'S ALL GOOD

Craig would see the priority of his family or that the video guy would get stronger in his faith and commitment. I wish I had prayed for my resolve to put me away and put God out front. I'm not beating myself up for all that; it's just sometimes we learn hard lessons as we reflect on the things we should've done.

It seemed everyone who was about to go on this tour was in a state of rebuilding in some way. I was an ex-drunk, ex-television producer who had just relocated to Grand Rapids, Michigan. Craig had just moved the ministry and entire family to GR as well. The video guy had a new career, baby, and half-built house.

Then there was Dave the Driver. He literally had nothing when he stepped on the RV. He carried a small red duffel bag … that's it. Dave spent years killing himself with drugs and booze, and years trying to collect himself and live the "normal life." Months before the tour he called my cell phone, asking for a little help. He needed a place to stay while he rebuilt. Di and I were all too happy to have him. Little did we realize that we'd dream up the Starving Jesus Tour and would need a driver. Dave, as God would direct it, is a professional driver and skilled painter.

Dave has been my best friend since I can remember being alive. We had seen each other grow, make mistakes, and have successes. Starving Jesus was a perfect fit for a guy who needed something to get involved in and restart his life. Starving Jesus was beginning to be more than a book or a tour. It was giving people purpose and passion. It was allowing folks to define their faith. We were all ready to start … and finish. We were ready to see this project change lives.

Dave was making it possible for all of us to understand sacrifice. He was placing his entire life on the line as he went on tour. He had nothing lined up afterward; he had no sunset waiting for him in New York. Dave knew he should go and forgo the future for his faith in God.

Craig and I were prepared for some kind of sacrifice as well. Oftentimes the church seems quick to point out that our everyday lives are reason enough for not doing something ... anything. The tour was moving us away from family. We were worrying about them and what would happen. For us, it was a stopgap. When was the last time God showed you an opportunity and you faced it without cause or condition for its end, even if it meant leaving your family?

When was the last time you just went, because the end *did* justify the means? I can hear people yelling at me, "But, J.R., tell that to my kids when they are growing up without a father or mother because I was away being a good little disciple." Doing doesn't mean stupidity. We can be great parents and serve Christ; discernment is the answer to the equation. We are to grow ever more powerful as disciples of Christ with our walk and sacrifice. This means hard decisions will be made. Decisions that will question your faith, or lack thereof. It's not that your family isn't important; it's that your family is the most important. When you act out your faith, your family benefits from your obedience.

Dear friend, you are faithful in what you are doing   3 JOHN 5-8
for the brothers, even though they are strangers to
you. They have told the church about your love. You
will do well to send them on their way in a manner
worthy of God. It was for the sake of the Name that
they went out, receiving no help from the pagans.
We ought therefore to show hospitality to such men
so that we may work together for the truth.

There it was. A finished book, some money raised—not a   9.7
lot but enough to get us to San Francisco. We had our   OTHERS
crew, a schedule built for rock stars, and our wives would
join us periodically along the way. We were smart enough
to build in wife time. We re-upped our living wills, made

sure the lawns and bills would be taken care of, and ate like crazy as the days peeled away toward August 5, 2006.

We were working feverishly behind the scenes. Part of the cool thing we were doing was making sure every city had tangible ideas for outreach. We wanted everyone to have an opportunity to serve locally. The Starving Jesus Web site became a clearinghouse for groups and ministries that needed help or volunteers.

Brandon, the XXXchurch intern, was working day and night on assembling this warehouse of information. We created forty blogs on the site—one for each tour stop— and every blog had five tangible organizations that people could plug in to.

Brandon contacted each organization, built a relationship with them, and ultimately pushed them into the spotlight as we headed out on the road. It was our goal to either *do* outreach in every city or *inspire* outreach. The work Brandon did set the ball rolling.

J.R. was coordinating with every church: times, locations, the need-to-know info. It was amazing, as each city started to chime in with ideas. For example, Mission Year, the ministry we were visiting in Oakland, California, had us hopping from one outreach to the next. First, we fed old folks in a predominantly Asian neighborhood; then we visited a community-sponsored secondhand store in one the most violent areas in Oakland.

We had churches doing bike outreaches in city ghettos. Others were feeding the homeless, washing cars in apartment complexes, clothing expectant mothers; and one city tour was going to make sure five thousand kids got backpacks and school supplies for the upcoming school year.

We were simply overwhelmed as each of the forty churches answered the call, stepped up, and helped its community. A lot of times we were in absolute wonder when we realized we didn't have to do a lot with this except show up. J.R., Brandon, and I wouldn't have had the fortitude to plan, execute, or pull this thing off if it weren't solely for God's massive grace in our lives. It was simply humbling.

I have seen the burden God has laid on men. He has made everything beautiful in its time. He has also set eternity in the hearts of men; yet they cannot fathom what God has done from beginning to end.

ECCLESIASTES 3:10-11

The last of the details were set, and we started to pack as August 5 crept toward us. We were excited, afraid, generally filled with anxiety. We gathered for prayer a few days before we left. It was nice. The wives, a few friends— we prayed for about twenty minutes, everyone asking for safety on the road and a safe return home. Except for Dave the Driver. Dave has this wisdom that only comes from a life rebuilt. He asked something of God I was remiss in even thinking about. "God," he said quietly and very sincerely, "please impress on us the value this will take on in others' lives." He didn't ask for selfish ends; Dave asked God to help us humbly submit ourselves to those we would meet along the way. We hadn't even climbed into the RV yet, but Dave was already driving.

9.8
HERE WE COME

Starving Jesus went from crazy rant to physical outreach. Were we ready? How do you prepare? How do you know if it's the right direction? Is there a course offered on doing this? Is this foolishness? Would we manage to make an impact? Would the church hear us? Would our wives hate us by the end of this thing?

In the beginning God created the heavens and the earth.

GENESIS 1:1

There we were, day one, sitting chained to a pew in front of the Golden Gate Bridge. J.R. grinning like Benny Hinn;

9.9
DAY ONE

he was in his glory. The country right in front of us, and not one of us knew what we were doing. Not one! We had no backers, no crazy million-dollar support-check story, no one telling us what to do. Just four guys and one message: "Get up, get out!"

CH 10 | BEST OF THE WORST

Those who know your name will trust in you,
*   for you, Lord, have never forsaken those who seek*
you.

So there we were, beginning life in an RV for forty days, not quite sure if it was the right thing to do. We left our families to fend for themselves and were praying for the tour to touch someone and inspire the American church to ... just do. I was optimistic, to say the least, perhaps a little faithless really, as I pictured revival at the end of my hands.

10.1
IT'S ALL THE
SAME OUT
HERE

It's all the same in America: FedEx trucks, endless miles of strip malls, McDonald's and Waffle House restaurants, La Quintas, Days Inns. From California to New York, it's all the same. The originality of highways like Route 66 went out the door when four-lane superhighways, drive-throughs, brand marketing, rest stops, and vending machines were born. The superhighways of the '60s drove the entire country away from the fun of traveling and made way for the mass replication of bad taste. Getting off the highway today is more like a long wait for a crappy Disneyland ride. No more buried Cadillacs or restaurants shaped like shoes or the world's largest prairie dog museums. It's all gone; it's all a shame. Now we count Volkswagens until we arrive at Six Flags or hotel water parks. Not only are we starving Jesus, we're also starving imaginations.

Beyond my grousing about the romanticism of the road, people always surprise me. From city to city, I met the most sincere and caring people on the planet. I found myself not wanting to leave them and mourning them when I did. I will never forget John from Albuquerque, Rob from Wichita, Danny and Jamie in New Orleans, Mike and Jesse in Birmingham, Ollie in Georgia, and J.C.'s mansion in

Nashville. These are just a few. When we started this madness, I truly thought Christians had cashed it in. But when we were out there, instead of my expectations being met, I was consistently being proved wrong. Here were people, who didn't know us from Adam, willing to meet us along the way. They literally rolled out the red carpet, embraced us, loved us, and did everything short of wash and clean the RV—although a few did that, too.

ISAIAH 58:5-7

Is this the kind of fast I have chosen,
only a day for a man to humble himself?
Is it only for bowing one's head like a reed
and for lying on sackcloth and ashes?
Is that what you call a fast,
a day acceptable to the Lord?
Is not this the kind of fasting I have chosen:
to loose the chains of injustice
and untie the cords of the yoke,
to set the oppressed free
and break every yoke?
Is it not to share your food with the hungry
and to provide the poor wanderer with shelter—
when you see the naked, to clothe him,
and not to turn away from your own flesh and
blood?

10.2
ROCK STAR
MEETS CIRCUS
PERFORMER

Our day-to-day routine on tour fell into place during the first few days. It was like having a new girlfriend, or what I can remember it being like, anyway. So much to understand. So many places you just can't go, and so many places you can't wait to see.

We asked every church if they could help with a hotel room. We had enough forethought to know forty days in the RV would be ludicrous. The hotels would break up the monotony. Churches were more than happy to accommodate. We were truly grateful for that.

We were constantly battling directions. Between J.R., Dave the Driver, and our Magellan "Never Lost" satellite system, it was as if straight lines never existed. Our places in the RV took on the regularity of any kindergarten class. J.R. in the front passenger seat, Dave the Driver, well ... I liked the table/bed in the back, and our video guy wandered. Moving away from these coveted spots was problematic. It was funny—grown men protecting "their" seats like dogs would their bones. We settled in, dug in, and quickly discerned this was going to be a long journey. No food, a thirty-one-foot living compartment/box on wheels, and four guys who are not shy about sharing bodily gases. Ahhh ... the picture of modern-day discipleship.

We drove all night, chained ourselves to the pew in the morning, did some form of outreach during the day, and spoke at night. We found a rhythm in the routine, but it never took away from the fact that we solidly put ourselves out. Out in the middle of a subculture that was either geeked to see us or didn't much care that two guys were chaining themselves to a pew and not eating. Definitely to be expected.

The media loved us, which was cool. We managed to get press almost every place we visited. The press drove the message as we spit out sound bites like "Church is lazy." It was awesome knowing a few thousand people would hear about Starving Jesus. As a result, maybe people would come out to see us or hear us speak, maybe not. Either way we were issuing the challenge and praying it sank in.

Our crowds, well ... let's just say they varied. From sixteen hundred one night to eight another. Church crowds are fickle. If you're having an event on any other day besides Sunday or Wednesday, you're taking your chances. For us it meant these church staffs had to work a little harder to get the word out. For some this proved too much; for others it was like watching a group prepare for a presidential visit. From background checks to security, we were blown away with the hospitality of folks.

All in all the Starving Jesus Tour was like rock star meets circus performer meets Jesus freak meets regular American guy. An odd mix of subcultural celebrity and prayerful endeavoring.

Before we got on the road, my dad said this was the dumbest thing I would ever do. So much for the support. He would later recant his statement, only after seeing the produced fruit of an incredible journey. In some ways the tour was nuts, insane, completely out of the bounds of modern-day reality; and in other ways, it was genius, radical, and the best thing any of us would ever do. We put our money where our mouths were.

Beyond the meet and greets, the inspired outreaches, and long hours of tedious driving, there was this fast, which I had only tried once in my life and cheated. I was at a youth gathering. We were doing a twenty-four-hour famine. I slipped in a few cookies and chips as the kids did their thing. Who could blame me? I had seventy kids to look after. J.R. was completely jacked up about doing another forty-day fast, and I agreed forty days would be the right thing to do as we launched out on the road.

Understand, I don't have a lot of body fat to begin with (translation: I'm skinny). Everyone around me was concerned how this fast would look on me. My wife was afraid I would die, and J.R. wouldn't shut up about drinking tons of water.

Frankly, the whole thing freaked me out a little. I researched the subject like crazy. I was looking for ways to supplement the food in line with fasting food, of course, for example, juice concoctions and protein shakes. I knew a few people besides J.R. who had fasted long periods, and they seemed to do all right. One guy I know drank syrup, honey, and cayenne pepper while fasting. Sounded great until I mixed the three and drank it…. I about puked.

I settled on juice smoothies and high-protein drinks; J.R., water and juice.

I guess I was expecting some weird form of spirituality to fall from the sky. J.R. was filled with stories from his first forty-day fast, and truthfully, I was hoping some of that would fall on me. The thing is, fasting works different for everyone. God meets you when you fast. He met me right away, not some other guy who needed a good shot in the arm about his priorities with family, work, and friends. I opened my eyes somewhere between LA and New York. My fast had nothing to do with J.R.'s experience. I heard J.R.'s rhetoric about fasting, but understanding that my fast looked, sounded, and felt completely different from everyone else's was a revelation. I was looking for the same effect as J.R.'s fast or my California buddy's fast or even Jesus' fast. It didn't happen. And then I saw what my wife and family were going through as my fast toiled on. Even as J.R. fell apart right in front of me, God literally directed my eyes to the most important things in my life. He held a magnifying glass up for me, saying, *Take a look. What ya think?* and *What ya want to change or keep the same?* He was uncomfortably close. And the crazy thing? It was affecting everyone around me. The fast consumed my life and, in doing so, spoke to everyone within my reach.

Here is a trustworthy saying that deserves full ac-   1 TIMOTHY
ceptance: Christ Jesus came into the world to save   1:15-16
sinners—of whom I am the worst. But for that very
reason I was shown mercy so that in me, the worst
of sinners, Christ Jesus might display his unlimited
patience as an example for those who would believe
on him and receive eternal life.

Honestly, this chapter hurts to write, but it's me. I owe God   10.3
the action of being honest with you. He changed me. You   GOOD
need to know that. You can disseminate the information   EXAMPLE, J.R.

and its sincerity any way you like; fasting and a tour with three other guys will bear out this type of honesty. It is also pertinent to understand that honesty and truth are two different things. Honesty is momentary. Truth is eternal. So I can say very honestly, I will continue to change as this ride continues; stay with me for updates.

The hardest thing for any Christian? Seeking God day to day. As you do, he will mirror you. Your life will either change for him or fade away into the large crowds that gather every Sunday.

I got on that stinking RV on August 5, 2006, thinking I was the best. After all, I conceptualized Starving Jesus, I skinned this thing with its rhetoric, and I am the older, wiser of the punks I was traveling with.

My ego hung out on a line for all to see. I could answer every question. I could counsel every problem, and I could navigate the country without help. After all, I am J.R.

Paul might have penned it first, but I personified the thought: I am the worst of the sinners. Right away I was having personality conflicts with everyone in the RV. I was treating my friend Dave the Driver as if he were a child. Craig became opposition no matter what the discussion. We actually argued about time zones. The video guy was just an annoyance as he asked five hundred questions an hour about the tour and the reality of Christ for the film.

Along the way we would arrive at an outreach, church, or speaking gig; and I would turn into Moses. I would speak gently, quietly, with strength and assurance; and I had all the answers and was willing to expand your knowledge of my greatness. My friends back in the newsroom have a name for that kind of behavior. I know a few Christians who also know that name.

I was right ... all the time. Don't challenge me. Give me the respect I am owed and, for God's sake, understand that I am the giver of this remarkable book and tour. I was an idiot! Plain and simple.

I wouldn't start recognizing this behavior until day thirteen of the tour. It's not that I was completely in the dark about my issues with an overextended ego and a vengeful sense of pride. These wonderful traits have haunted me like a crack habit my entire life. I have done everything imaginable to keep them comfortably in check, and for the most part, I had been moderately successful, with the exception of a few damaged relationships here and there. But a fast without change isn't a fast.

The tour from anyone's vantage point was not pleasant, as you can imagine. I certainly didn't count on my demise, nor did anyone else. It's actually quite simple why I lost control. Sin. I was literally lost in the sin of pride. I was thinking I had something revolutionary to say and do. I was lost in the thought that I mattered to the process, that I needed to be heard, and that I needed to be propped up. If I was questioned or shown a lack of respect, I went nuts. If I thought I was not getting credit, I would attack.

Simply put: I was lost. It's ironic, too, because at no other time in my walk with Christ had I felt so strong and secure in my faith than the months leading up to the tour. How must Simon Peter have felt after the Lord called him Satan? Let me tell you. It doesn't feel good, nor does it remember well.

In my life I have been addicted to drugs, booze, coffee, and now … me. The hardest thing I have ever faced, the most disgusting detoxification I have ever endured: me. No rehab in the world was capable of taking on this mess. Only Christ and an RV full of guys. I was the worst of the best.

I sometimes think it's a shame my pride rose and fell on the Starving Jesus Tour, or perhaps the tour was designed for that kind of crap. I'm still flushing it out.

The reality of my sin was felt at the expense of those in that RV. Fasting is not pleasurable for the sinner; it's joyous for those praying for change, but it ain't like a party for those in the middle of it. I am sure there were prayers asking God for my eyes to be clear. I thank God for those prayers and the willingness of others to forgive.

Here is something I wrote during the second week of the tour. It speaks for itself.

August 13, 2006

I find it incredibly hard to get along with everyone on the RV. We are in closed confining quarters and the personalities in this RV are all very strong. Arguments over everything seem to crop up at the most inconvenient times. Everything from what was said an hour ago to what the Bible says about Revelation. In the end, this is a lesson of forgiveness.

An adjustment must be made in order to not cover the same the ground again. I am working diligently on not braking, bossing, or controlling people around me. This behavior has haunted me for some time. On this forty-day fast God is pulling me away from always having to be out front, always having to be in control, always having to be right, always having something to say. I am seeing myself daily, and it can be a big drag but something that needs to happen. I find myself at the end of the day in a giant state of forgiveness with God. Asking him to forgive me, screaming, "I am sorry!" for the behaviors that drive me away from him and me away from the people in my life. I am selfish, self-centered, and downright hypocritical. That is me, this is my fast. It is what it is, and I will accept these shortcomings in light of the other side and what that will mean as God helps me deal with the crap in my life. I am not proud of these traits nor do I welcome them. I truly wish them dead.

I am reading John's gospel throughout this fast. I see an apostle of great love and understanding for Christ. John was beloved to Jesus; he must have been something else. I imagine him watching Jesus, asking him questions about the why and how of it all. I imagine the wide-eyed looks at Jesus as he changed the planet with his answers and actions.

Day thirteen proved that the fast was full on. In John 3:30, John the Baptist lets it go very easily with one big fat put-yourself-away assertion: "He must become greater; I must become less." For me and this RV, it's that way. I am the guy who competes, wants to get it right the first time. Be first every time. I struggle with the possibilities of my own fame. My actions oftentimes only glorify me. Whether I like it or not, he must be greater than me, and I must become less. My lessons on this RV? Simple. Put myself away and serve those around me. I have spent so much time seeking my own assurance, I forgot about those around me. Forgive me, Lord. Forgive me, my friends.

My family, my friends. I am thinking they do a better job at being a part of my life than I, them. The reciprocation frankly wanes on my side of the fence. I know I am a big voice for those around me who on occasion need a push or prod, but I also realize that voice translates into my thinking I am somehow ahead of the game. Not true, just my crazy, sinful thinking driving a spectacular ego and pride the likes of which can smash and divide. This fast is an exercise. A painful strip of isolation in a place where I must be on top of my game every day. I am in a position to lead people, and I must step it up. My foul mouth must be tamed, my sinful pride must be quieted, and I must find a place where I find solace with God concerning these behaviors. I don't have a problem letting you know. I know one thing for sure: Honesty leads to maturity, and the return on maturity is immeasurable amounts of peace in my life.

I suppose this is a diatribe of all the crazy stuff in my life. I suppose people could read this and wonder why one would want that much self-examination. Well … peace with God and peace with you. It's a solid testimony for others to see a guy who so desperately needs and wants change.

Forty days, no food, a trip across the country, and the one thing that finally broke me in half? ... One sentence from Clint, our XXXchurch Web designer. He was on the tour for a few stops, helping shoot the documentary. The video guy was shooting interviews, and he asked Clint what he thought about the fast and me. Clint was honest and sincere when he answered: "After watching J.R.'s example, I don't think I will ever fast."

PROVERBS 1:5 *Let the wise listen and add to their learning,*
and let the discerning get guidance.

10.4 I was lying on my back and had just been told to take a
ONLY 30 deep breath. The doctor said I would have a warm sensation in my body and a funny taste in my mouth. That was from the X-ray blood dye just inserted into an IV going into my body. This was my first trip to the emergency room since tenth grade, and it wasn't how I envisioned spending the first full day back from tour. I was fifteen minutes away from finding out what was causing the pain in my heart. The reason I needed a scan was that the doctor thought I was at risk for a blood clot or, possibly, there was something wrong with my heart. The scan was simple; the hard part came fifteen minutes later when the doctor returned to my hospital room to share the prognosis with me.

When I was under the scan, that verse rushed into my head. The verse I had been repeating for forty days once a night while on the SJ tour: Proverbs 1:5. J.R. and I would take the stage each night and share with people what God had been teaching us about church and faith. That verse will stick with me for the rest of my life.

The tour was simply unbelievable. It sparked my imagination and refreshed my spirit about church, all it is and all it still could be. We were involved in some great outreaches from a fix-your-bike outreach in the inner city of Houston to sharing Christ with prostitutes on some random street corner in Alabama.

God speaks. He has his way. Sometimes he does not speak loud enough, tell us as much as we want—or even what we need—to know. We decided to deny our bodies food for forty days and just drink juice, water, and other strange drinks. It was our way to plug in and listen.

I don't think God cares if you do forty days or forty hours, food or TV. He wants you. In giving up something, you will find him.

I went into the Starving Jesus Tour scared. I didn't want to end up in some clinic outside Phoenix with Mary-Kate Olsen, starving, looking for a wafer. I only weigh 145 pounds, and that's soaking wet. I knew I could handle not eating, but what was God going to say to me? What was God going to do in my life and the lives of those around me for forty days?

I thought God would speak louder as I was fasting. After all, it was God who was guiding this foodless effort. I was waiting for a burning bush or maybe lightning flashes.

The simple fact: He meets you as you seek him. Fast or no fast, you draw close to him; he draws close to you. With that said, there's nothing wrong with a good old-fashioned fast. In Matthew 6, it doesn't say Christ fasted to give you an idea of something to do on your day off. God's looking for participation, active participation with him as you live day to day. Occasionally, fasting should be a part of that day to day.

Pretty simple, but it took me about twenty or so days to understand it. I heard things, I paid attention to things, things stuck with me, things happened that, in my everyday life, I would have just passed over, but instead I hung on to them, and it was those things that brought me through the fast: a few moments I will never forget and moments that will bring me back to the fast.

God showed me he is in charge. God showed me that everything I have is his because of him. God put me in an RV I could not drive that traveled 10,790 miles across the United States. That taught me patience. Being stuck in that RV, sometimes driving in circles, not being able to find our next location, would normally drive me nuts, but I got used to it. I had to, because that was life for forty days. I was reminded to slow down and just enjoy everything: my family, my friends, and all that God is doing. I am only thirty, but it just seems like life is going too fast. Life did not stop for me on that RV, but in a sense, it almost did. Every day we did just about the same thing, and throughout it all, I found where my priorities need to be.

Early on the trip, a pastor in Kansas shared a random quote with me on a walk outside the church. "Don't cheat your family, Craig; cheat the church." I held on to that one.

As I lay there, I thought about day twenty-seven. That was the night I received a phone call I will never forget. I can't stand prosperity preachers and don't buy it at all. God does not promise cash if you fast. God will do something, but becoming a banker isn't one of them. I went into the fast hoping God would do for me what he did for J.R. Wrong. What I needed, I got. What J.R. needed, he got.

J.R. came to work for XXXchurch in 2006, and I had just moved my family to Grand Rapids from California. It was tough. I knew God told me to move. He wanted me to put my time and energy into the ministry and build XXXchurch.com. My mission was clear. I knew that meant I had to hire J.R. full-time. It was a no-brainer, except now the ministry had to pay him. On top of that, J.R. and I birthed Starving Jesus, which, when all was said and done, was costing the ministry over $50,000 and would not bring in revenue for some time. So … was money going to show up at the front door like it did for Kirk Cameron on *Growing Pains?* Not only did I not think it would, I did not even think or pray for it. Funny how the desires of our heart can often go unattended in prayer and still stick like glue in our lives.

Jeremiah 29:11 says, "'For I know the plans I have for you,' declares the Lord, 'plans to prosper you and not to harm you, plans to give you hope and a future.'"

The phone call came from a friend. His church wanted to financially sow into our ministry. He told me they wanted to divide it up in monthly payments. By the way, we get paid monthly. My friend told me the amount they wanted to give over the next twelve months. Do I even need to write this? Yes, the amount my friend had for the ministry is the exact amount XXXchurch would be paying J.R. The exact number! Not off by a dollar, a dime, a cent. Exactly! For God knows the plans ... *All right, God, I get it! I get it! I thought I got it back in California. But I get it now ... what is next, God? I moved my family across the country, hired staff, and headed out on a forty-day tour and fast. God, if you want me to go into space with Lance Bass, I am there.* Well, maybe not Lance Bass.

Those fifteen minutes in a hospital bed seemed to be more like an hour. *God,* I said while lying there, *I've got some heart murmur, and J.R. is now going to have to do this thing by himself. God, he's the forty-year-old— shouldn't he be the first to go?* These thoughts and prayers ran through me.

God, whatever news I get, I will be okay with, because I know you know the plans. I sensed God needed all those things to happen over the last year for me to come to a point where I believe that his plans are better than mine, and this heart condition would be my final test. I prayed, *Lord, whatever the case, you are in control ... thank you.*

I called my wife, as it seemed like a whole day had passed. She did not pick up her cell phone or the house phone. After all, I did drive myself to the emergency room and took my laptop into the hospital, in case I had some extra time. So she was not that worried. As she was calling me back, I quickly hit silence on the phone as the head doctor entered into room 14. He peeked his head into my room and proceeded to pull up a chair right next to my bed.

He said, "You're fine.... Now explain this trip to me."

GENESIS 4:6-7   *Then the Lord said to Cain, "Why are you angry? Why is your face downcast? If you do what is right, will you not be accepted? But if you do not do what is right, sin is crouching at your door; it desires to have you, but you must master it."*

10.5   I wrote this a few days after the tour:

AFTER ALL

Pained and gripped with fear, I prayed out loud. "Lord," I say very quietly, "I know there will be another fast. I know it will refine me, retool me, break me. But please, Lord, bring it to me slowly, gently, and most of all, with some warning." I look up and hope he hears my plea. I sit back quietly and think about the smell of the RV, the stickiness of the floor, the loud repetitive hum of the overworked engine. I smile and thank God for not being in the RV but for being here, in my house with my wife, who's in the next room where I can finally see her, touch her.

The tour kicked my butt. The travel, the fast ... In the end I was physically exhausted, emotionally spent, and spiritually drained from the constant mirroring of behaviors and actions.

The moon is blasting into the room I am hiding out in. It is peaceful, I am happy, no stops to make, no one to greet, no one to meet, no hotel to find, no church to speak at, and no talk about praying, giving, or fasting. I should be more grateful for those forty days, but right now I simply am not. I am just happy to know when this prayer is over I can climb into bed with my wife and just sleep.

The tour opened me up in ways I will be discerning for the rest of my life. The fast alone was enough to bring me flat before the Lord, asking forgiveness for my actions, behaviors, and wicked tongue. The sad truth about me made its way to the Starving Jesus rooftop more than once inside the RV. "Lord," I say as I hang my head, "please give me strength to change, and please forgive me."

I think about all the outreach, all the selfless acts of kindness. I think about all the new friends I made along the way ... like John, Gabriel, Ben, Danny, TJ, Josh, Mike, Sean, Ron, Erin, Jamie, Hector, Rob, John Jay, JC, Demo, Kim, Jake, Graydon, Ryan, Christian, Eric, Zane, Mark, Sammy D, Jeremiah, Brent, Erich, Pastor Mike, Doug, and Paul.

I pray hard for these people, because these people are getting it done. I think about the countless number of homeless, broken, and wandering people we met along the way who stopped and talked with us about their immediate needs. I am so proud of our entire team who stepped up and met everyone with love and dignity. "This is how I want to live my life, Lord," I say out loud. "This is how I want to live my life ... Lord." I repeat it slowly so he hears me and he does, I know he does. "Thank you, Lord, for the tour ... even the stinky, sticky, loud, stupid RV. Thank you for breaking me during the fast, thank you for the examples along the way, and Lord ... thank you for proving me wrong. Amen."

I get up slowly, as I am forty, fumble through the dark, find my way into the bedroom and flop down alongside my wife and giggle like a girl. "What's so funny?" Di asks.

"Nothing, just so happy to be here. Good night, baby."

"I'm glad you're home," she says quietly. She grabs my hand, and we fall asleep like some kind of movie. It's quite nice.

Starving Jesus

The Starving Jesus Tour defined itself by change. In the end, we had very little to do with that. We will no doubt be hearing and telling stories about that forty days for a lifetime. You do not fast simply; the time and intentions must be there. It bears itself out in the stories of one human being doing for another: stories of hope, fulfillment, and new beginnings. It's your story, my story. The stories of people we don't know. Ultimately, God asks us to do something, and we obey. We go forward, forsaking those around us, so we can change, love, and forgive.

CH 11 | FAT MAN STARVING

"Even now," declares the Lord,
"return to me with all your heart,
with fasting and weeping and mourning."

JOEL 2:12

You have to decide. Decide what following Jesus means, or walk aimlessly. Christian or not, this is the search. We can debate it for hours, but that's all there is. Oftentimes the church gets lost in its meaning. We are always on the look-out for the next great idea, translation of Scripture, meaning, or new Christian thought. This book is a great example of that. What is *Starving Jesus* in this landscape? For us it's easy: Move people to give, fast, and pray. We couldn't care less about the interruption, translation, and general talk this line of thinking will produce. We care about the generated action it will produce.

J.R. and I like to measure success with stories (for those lost in the subculture, the testimonies). At the end of the day as J.R. and I sit back, the question is "What did we do as a result of this faith we have?" We understand that works aren't saving us or anyone else, for that matter, but works designed to inspire people to Christ will help answer the most important question in the world: Who is Jesus? The journey to that question means there will be another side as you answer.

We decided to live this thing out—hard—for everyone to see. This country has afforded us that opportunity. It's one thing for us to talk about it, but we are so convinced that in him the work makes sense. We must say something. It is our hope as we live this out that we inspire, challenge, and lead people to Christ.

Do you think J.R. and Rob had any clue what their first fast would mean? They couldn't see past day one.

Imagine launching out on a journey and having no clue

where you were going and every possibility of screwing it up. Would you go? Add to that equation being oblivious that everything you do would inspire others to do the same.

J.R. and Rob sat in a small cramped office, trying to pay the mortgage with a business they conceived from faith. They wanted to love God, honor him, and take care of their families. Fasting was their method to say, "Save us, God," and "You, God, are the only one who matters." They laid flat for God, prayed unceasingly for forty days, asked for change, listened, studied, and ultimately came to one conclusion: God is real. Rob and J.R. answered the question and, as a result, people have been led to ask the question of themselves.

As for me, Starving Jesus became the one way I will live my life. I will walk with him, because he is my life. Maybe that's a little more than perfunctory, but that's all it is and all it has to be.

GALATIANS 5:1 *It is for freedom that Christ has set us free. Stand firm, then, and do not let yourselves be burdened again by a yoke of slavery.*

11.2
NASCAR
WILLIE
In the end we haven't said anything new. Is this a rant or complaint? Perhaps. More to the point, it's two guys passionate about what we love and how we express that love. We don't want to be Martin Luther or labeled crazy heretics, although we would be comfortable with either.

I suppose in some ways church will always suck—the politics, personalities, and mindless obsession with the number of converts. Church is sinful because we are sinful. We as a body are prone to wander from God; God doesn't wander from us. Craig and I are not reformers. We're just two guys trying desperately to stay humble while flushing out a message we feel is valuable and worthy of practice. I guarantee you three things: When you give, he will give back. When you fast, he will meet you. When you pray, he will find you.

Our friend Ollie from Georgia who went to Ukraine before the Starving Jesus Tour? He got it. He saw value in stepping out and living his faith. His Starving Jesus story didn't need its own book or cross-country tour with forty separate outreaches. Ollie's story just needed living examples that a life filled with faith was not going to make him nuts, crazy, or some freak.

Ollie was a children's pastor in the middle of Georgia. He was content living day to day, saying some prayers, shepherding his flock, and weighing in at 410 pounds. That's right! Ollie was 410 pounds. Was he supposed to be? No. Ollie told us his sin caught up with him. He had spent years running from the pain and hurt every human endures. His drive to run from God, truth, life, love, and salvation drove him to fill the gap with food. In the process, he alienated his wife, kids, family, congregation, and God.

If you were to have met Ollie, you would say, "Great guy!" Loving, trustworthy, great personality, loves God! All true, except for the weight of sin he was literally walking around in. Ollie, like everyone else on this planet, was in some form of constant running to or from sin. Ollie was a great example of a guy needing to give it all up, stop starving Jesus. What was so problematic was that he was a pastor! *The weight couldn't be about sin. He's a pastor! It's gotta be genetic or something wrong with his glands!* This is what you may have told yourself after meeting Ollie.

I had talked with Ollie one time as we went into the Starving Jesus Tour. He didn't sound like a guy with a big fat sin problem. He actually inspired me on the phone. He made me think twice about how I was serving people after he told me what he was up to in Ukraine.

Craig had said earlier that Ollie's church was just outside of Atlanta; I took his word for it. We headed into Atlanta on August 24. Our plan? Chain ourselves to the pew in Centennial Park. Centennial Park was built in the middle of Atlanta as an attraction for the 1996 Olympic Games. During the games it became the site of a deadly domestic terrorist bombing that killed 2 and injured 111. The world headquarters of CNN sits on one corner of the park as well. The location was ideal for two guys to chain themselves to a pew.

As we were finding a place to park the RV, I quickly checked the map to see how much time we needed to get to Ollie's church after we were done acting like idiots. I was thinking a forty-minute drive, tops, if the church was "just outside of Atlanta." Turns out Ollie's church sits in Byron, Georgia, a small town *not* just outside of Atlanta, but for most people, a day's drive outside of Atlanta: ninety-three miles, to be precise. Craig needs some kind of rehab for those struggling geographically. Bottom line: We would have to wait even longer to see our wives that night.

After we spoke at Ollie's church, the plan was to head to the Atlanta airport and pick up our wives, who were flying in from Grand Rapids. It was going to be the first time I saw Diane in twenty days. For Craig it would be the second time he was to see Jeanette and the kids; no matter ... seeing the wives any time on this trip was fantastic. When I figured out we would miss them at the airport because Gross was no Magellan, I was, to say the least, upset.

Here we were in Atlanta, unloading the pew, tired, and exhausted. We hadn't eaten in twenty days because of the fast and hadn't slept well in twenty days because of the grueling travel schedule. The tour was literally killing us. We kept the harsh physicality of this tour to ourselves most of the time and put a good face on. But seriously, it got so bad for us we found it almost impossible to lift the pew or carry our own luggage at the end of the day, let alone speak to a few hundred people, then hang out until eleven o'clock at night, talking and praying with people after an event. Most nights we would get back to the hotel at midnight, get three, maybe four hours of sleep, and then *bam!* be back out the door for the next city. Sometimes we skipped the hotels altogether in lieu of driving all night, because we had an early outreach the next day. Sleeping in an RV is like sleeping in the rain: You don't sleep.

Dave the Driver was exhausted as well. Not only was he driving all day and night, but he was our tour manager. This meant he was in charge of all the Compassion Kid tables, the pew set, book and video sales, and the general tour management stuff. From handling the money to getting to each city and dealing with the waste we produced on the RV, this was not a glamorous job. He didn't raise an eyebrow; in fact, I don't think he complained once. If he were Catholic, Dave would be in the running to be canonized when he dies.

Centennial Park went exactly as we planned. The local NBC station showed up, we did a little TV, it was all good. We jumped on the RV. We weren't the happiest of campers as we headed to Ollie's church, but nonetheless, off we went.

I imagined Byron, Georgia, like Mayberry: one gas station, a sheriff with no gun. It turns out Byron has a lot going on. First and foremost, Byron has three Waffle House restaurants, two on I-75 exits to Byron and one just outside of town. The greatest quality Byron has? Ollie.

As we pulled up to Ollie's church, it was evident something was going on at this place. It was a new building, looked nice, had a cute little waterfall treatment outside the front door. Inside it was very modern and clean. *These people must do church well,* I thought.

Up until we arrived at Ollie's church, we were getting some pretty good crowds. Ranging from one hundred people to fifteen hundred people on any given day. Generally, we wanted to see one hundred people at each event or outreach, and generally we were happy with the crowds that joined us during the Starving Jesus Tour.

We walked into Ollie's church with about forty-five minutes to spare before Craig and I were slated to speak. We stood in the lobby for about five minutes. The place was dark, quiet, and cold. No one running around, no one greeting us. I double-checked the church name and address.

Usually churches rolled out the red carpet; not that they had to, they just did. Maybe here not so much? I got nervous. Had I messed up the date? Was Ollie dead in the back and the killer still on the loose? I had no idea. When I talked with him the day before on the phone, he said, "We're all set to go," in that trailer-park southern accent I have grown to love.

We wandered around the church, finally found an office door open, and sitting at a desk in the corner was a tall lengthy guy. "You Ollie?" I asked cautiously as the tall guy got up and hurried over to see us. "You must be the Starving Jesus boys," the big guy said with a huge grin on his face. "I'm Ollie."

"Dude! Are we at the right place for the event?" Craig chimed in.

"This is it ... I hope we get some people out tonight. What time is it anyway?"

Great! I'm thinking. *We have to wait to see our wives so we can watch NASCAR Willie here call everyone in Byron to see if they're coming tonight.* I turn to Craig as we headed out the door to drag in the pew: "We should have canceled this gig."

"You think?" Craig says.

At that moment, it felt as if we should have entered Byron, Georgia, and kept on driving. We were fifteen minutes from start time and had no one from the church who could run the videos or PowerPoint for the Starving Jesus talk, and to cap it all off, there were only eight people sitting in the back row of the sanctuary—eight!

PROVERBS 21:3 *To do what is right and just is more acceptable to the Lord than sacrifice.*

11.3
WHO IS THAT? I need to interject a little information here. I do a lot of speaking around the country. It's a really awesome thing God has given me and a great opportunity to meet people.

In February 2006, Mars Hill Bible Church in Grand Rapids asked me to speak. I taught on a chapter right out of this book, "Ignorable Calling." The idea behind the talk and chapter was that as the body of Christ we can't continue ignoring God. I spoke a lot about J.R.'s first fast and what he and Rob had gone through as they crossed the finish line on a forty-day fast.

What I didn't realize at the time was the number of people who download the Mars Hill sermons every week. For the record, it's a lot. My e-mail box was packed for weeks from people who wanted more info on fasting and taking that next step. J.R. and I had no clue that the fast and that sermon would wind up in the ears of people who would actually step up to the plate, fast, and change their lives. We couldn't have predicted the response, even on our most prideful days.

I wandered back into the office where Ollie was camped out. He put on a great spread for those eating on tour. He had barbeque and corn bread for Dave the Driver and the video guy. I started to get really curious about this guy. He wasn't very engaged in the whole thing and looked kind of nervous, almost shifty. I looked around the office for whatever. Hanging on one of the walls were about ten framed family portraits. A nice-looking family: a beautiful blonde woman, two very cute little girls, and a real big, fat guy. Something about the fat guy in the photos was really familiar. I assumed it was Ollie's brother. "Who's this, your brother's family?" I say. Ollie's sitting on the couch, watching Dave the Driver gorge himself on barbeque, and then stands up and walks over to the row of pictures.

"No, that's my family," he says very sincerely.

"Who's the guy with them?"

"That's me."

"Come on! There's no way that's you." I stood in complete disbelief. The guy in front of me answering questions was not the guy in the pictures.

"Yep, that's me about 150 pounds ago," says Ollie.

"Are you serious?"

"Drop-dead serious."

I had to look five times, then relook, and look again. Then I prayed and ran and got J.R. Even as I write this, I still can't believe the pictures in his office were of the same guy I had just met that day, August 24, 2006. It was like two different guys.

I go get J.R. "Dude, you have to see this. Ollie lost 150 pounds! He was 410 pounds a few months ago. The pictures will trip you out."

We gather in the office ten minutes before the gig, and Ollie rolls out his story. "About a year ago I was a few days away from a full gastric bypass surgery. I was the most miserable, depressed guy in the world. I had to eliminate the weight, or I was going to die. I could barely walk, couldn't get on an airplane without help, couldn't do the simplest things with my family. Life basically sucked, and I was ashamed of myself and ashamed I had let my life get to that point."

Ollie had tried everything. Every diet, every prayer, every piece of advice. Even his current position as children's pastor couldn't help him, nothing seemed to work. We were all dead silent, listening to his story. He looked us straight in the eyes: "If it weren't for you guys, who knows what would have happened."

PROVERBS
3:7-8

Do not be wise in your own eyes;
   fear the Lord and shun evil.
This will bring health to your body
   and nourishment to your bones.

11.4
THE STORY OF
STARVING
JESUS

We were minutes from doing this gig in Byron, there were eight people in the audience, no church video guy for the presentation, and Ollie just told us we helped save his life. Speechless, aghast, thunderstruck, dazed, and tongue-tied, I got up on stage and chained myself to the pew.

We did the gig as if there were five thousand people lis-tening, one of our best, I might say. When Craig and I would speak every night on tour, we did a tag-team thing. He would accentuate one point, and I another. One of us was always sitting in the pew while the other was "preach-ing." After twenty days of the same talk, you begin to let your mind wander while the other is speaking. Ollie's church was no different. When I wasn't talking, I was try-ing to figure out where Ollie's 150 pounds went.

In those minutes before we took the stage Ollie went on to say, "When I heard Craig's sermon about you and Rob fasting forty days, I decided to do the same thing. So I fasted. When I started, I was 410 pounds. I was miserable, yet I heard God asking me to step out. I heard him ask for me, all of me."

As I was listening to Ollie, I was extremely nervous, even though he was right in front of me. I couldn't help but think what would have happened to this guy's life. I mean, he was 410 pounds; the story was so totally insane. I knew enough about fasting that if Ollie were in it with the Lord, actively seeking him in prayer and study, then God would take care of him. His fast was just so radical. I mean, it's one thing to be a few pounds overweight, but a few hun-dred pounds. I mean, come on! Funny thing is, I had a physical example of the power and grace of God right in front of me, and I couldn't help but try and blow holes in the story. I'm asking the same questions people asked me who couldn't believe that I had fasted for forty days, let alone the tour and second fast.

"You ate no food?" I asked, as if I was going to catch him in a big fat lie.

"No food," Ollie said confidently.

"You went forty days?"

"Yeah!"

"Did everyone around you know? Did you tell a doctor? Did you—"

He stopped me. "Water and juice, just like you … and

everyone knew." Ollie literally steps up in the office and holds court. "In August of 2005 I went on a business trip and had to fly. I'd never flown commercially before. I'll never forget sitting in the seat and not being able to buckle the belt. I had to ask the flight attendant, in front of other passengers, for a seat-belt extender. It was humiliating. During this trip, I flew on three different planes and had to get the belt extender on each plane.

"In November of 2005, our pastor, Joe, and I met for a one-on-one leadership meeting. Joe told me he really felt like the next year could be the best year of my life; he said he thought God had told him that. That day I sat down and made a list of things that would need to happen for me to have the best year of my life. One of those things was to lose one hundred pounds, and I told Joe I was going to do that. But I didn't try to lose weight right away....

"In late February/early March of 2006, I was going through some stuff spiritually. I just felt like God was telling me he was going to do some new stuff in my life and that he wanted us to work on our relationship with each other. Well, as long as I've been a follower of Christ, even with my weight problem, I would always fast if I had a major decision or something big in my life. But the longest I had ever fasted was three or four days. But I kept thinking I should fast, and fast for real.

"I kept thinking about fasting, and praying about it, for a couple weeks. On March 18 I officiated at a wedding, and after the wedding, I went to get Cristi (my wife) and had some food. I took my iPod, because I wanted to listen to this podcast from Mars Hill. I had heard of XXXchurch and you guys, and this was when you were speaking at Mars Hill. In the podcast, you started talking about Rob and J.R. going on this forty-day fast.

"I was like, 'Okay, God, I keep thinking about fasting, I keep thinking you're telling me to fast, then I hear this guy talking about fasting. Okay, I'll do it.'

"When I got home, I told Cristi, 'I think I'm going to go

on a fast starting Monday.' She asked how long, and I said, 'Well, maybe a week, but I'm thinking forty days....' She kind of gave me a 'whatever' look.

"Oh yeah, at the wedding, I wore a size 60 long suit with size 56 pants ... and it wasn't very loose....

"That Monday, March 20, I started the fast—and I was miserable! I spent half the day standing at our church secretary's door, whining and complaining about how bad I felt. But the next day, I felt so good physically. And I really felt good for the whole fast. And spiritually, it wasn't like I was on my knees, praying nonstop day and night, but it was like I was praying all the time. It's like I was in this 24/7 mode of communication with God.

"I'll never forget one night I was walking down the stairs at the church, and God said, *You won't be children's pastor here much longer.* It was so real, but I was like, 'huh?'

"I was scheduled to go on a mission trip to Kiev, Ukraine, that July, and I spent a lot of time praying about the trip and what God wanted me to say to the people there during this fast. During the fast God was really teaching me he's the Creator and I'm the creation. He loves me and wants to be my Father. It was like I was able to make this connection that I'd never been able to make in my life.

"The fast ended April 29. My wife, Cristi, was away working a retreat, and, man, it was almost depressing for the fast to be over. I really thought about making the fast indefinite. I had noticed that my clothes were getting kind of loose but didn't really think that much about weight loss during the fast. I decided to see what size pants I could get into. I was able to wear size 50 pants (from a size 56 to a size 50 in forty days!).

"Then it hit me. I'd always thought I had no self-control. I thought losing weight was impossible for me, but God was like, *See, you had self-control for forty days; you can have self-control now.*

"I decided to start walking and just decided to eat really

light and pray about the stuff I ate ... kind of let God decide what I should eat. That first week after the fast, I walked one mile per day. It was tough at first, but then it got easier. I started walking really fast, and then I started adding distance to my walking. By the end of May, I was up to five miles of fast walking per day. I had set a goal of getting to size 42 pants by July 12, the day I would leave for Ukraine. Cristi went out and bought me a pair of size 42 jeans at Salvation Army. Once a week I'd try them on. The first week, I actually pulled them all the way up, but was like four inches from being able to button them. The next week, it was a little closer. Then, on the third week, on *June* 12, I actually buttoned the pants! I had gone from a size 56 on March 18 to a size 42 on June 12!

"I kept exercising and eating better. In early June I added running to my walking. I'd walk four miles, then jog two miles.

"On July 12, I left for Kiev. It was the most incredible feeling to get on the plane, sit down, buckle the seat belt, and even have to tighten it up!!! During the trip to Ukraine, God did so many incredible things! Before I went, I asked him what I should tell the people there. I asked him how to be culturally relevant to these kids in Kiev. He told me to just hug them and tell them that he is their Father and he loves them. So that's what I did, and it was like pouring water on a dry sponge. Almost every kid there told me they'd never gotten a hug from their dad. They said their dad had never told them he loved them or was proud of them. They were so amazed with the fact that God is their Father and he *loves them!*

"God told me while I was there that I was supposed to move to Kiev and start a church there. I had planned to fast along with the Starving Jesus Tour for forty days. Now it was like I really had something to pray about during this fast."

"So ... you're fasting now with us during the tour?" I asked.

"Umm, yeah, man!"

Ollie's life had changed. His relationship with his wife and kids was 180 degrees different. He could play again; he could ... well, enjoy his wife again. He was filled with joy. He was living the life God had intended, free from his sin.

I was literally without faith as Ollie was telling his story. I was Thomas in front of Jesus, looking for holes; I doubted the very thing that had changed my life. Ollie's story was real, true, inspiring, life changing, and had unbelievable consequences. His family changed forever, his church changed forever, and the country he would live in changed. I stood in front of him with disbelief. When you act out your faith, when you move toward God, it is often the hardest thing to comprehend, especially when it produces fruit you can touch, eat, and share. From nothing stems something. This is how God gets it done. But how can it be true? How can God, whom we have never seen, never heard, interact with us? How can God change our lives after the collection of garbage we manage to amass in a lifetime? Yet somehow when we step forward in a belief that says he can and will, he shows up and we come to understand he is our salvation, our hope, and our freedom from whatever sin takes us down. Neither Craig nor I—not even Ollie—had much to do with that 150-plus pounds coming off. God was solely responsible. Ollie's sin was met by God. Ollie stepped out, and God produced fruit where no fruit had grown. That combination will always be a mysterious reality with life-changing consequences the world can never deny.

His wife, Cristi, that extremely beautiful blonde in the pictures on his wall, had been sitting in the room the whole time, listening. I turned to question her and stopped. Cristi had this proud, proud look on her face. It was peaceful. It was confident. It was the look of a woman who had seen change in a man who perhaps she had conceded might never change. The look said, "That's my husband, that's my love, that's the man I married, that's the man who leads our family." I said nothing after that. Ollie looked at us and said, "Let's do it!" We walked out of the office.

We had no video that night. We had eight people in the chairs for the event. From the outside looking in, it was the worst stop on the tour. We missed some time with our wives and family. We were tired, beat, and hungry. The stop frankly made no sense; after all, wasn't it about filling the seats with people?

We said good-bye to Ollie and his wife. We climbed back on the RV somewhere after nine o'clock that night. I think we sponsored one Compassion child and received a fifty-dollar donation, which was about the cost of gas to get us to Byron from Atlanta. Dave the Driver was cruising back to the hotel as fast as that crappy RV could roll, so we could see our wives. We were all quiet. It had been a long day.

Ollie's story knocked the wind out of us. It brought us to our knees in more ways than one. Byron, Georgia, hadn't been the worst stop; it had become *the* stop. We didn't need explanations on why only eight showed up for the event or why we even met Ollie. It was pretty obvious. God needed the tour to take on a story that would change us. I was remembering Dave the Driver's prayer before we left. Dave had said, "Father, please impress on us the value this will take on in others' lives." That prayer was answered on day twenty for all of us. I got a little nervous.... *What's next, God?*

By the way, Ollie, his wife, and two kids left for Ukraine to live happily ever after in the spring of 2007. He will be wearing size 35 pants. If you need Ollie, find him at www.lifepointkiev.com.

REVELATION
22:21

The grace of the Lord Jesus be with God's people. Amen.

2 CORINTHIANS
11:24–29

Five times I received from the Jews the forty lashes minus one. Three times I was beaten with rods, once I was stoned, three times I was shipwrecked, I spent

a night and a day in the open sea, I have been con-
stantly on the move. I have been in danger from
rivers, in danger from bandits, in danger from my
own countrymen, in danger from Gentiles; in danger
in the city, in danger in the country, in danger at sea;
and in danger from false brothers. I have labored
and toiled and have often gone without sleep; I have
known hunger and thirst and have often gone with-
out food; I have been cold and naked. Besides
everything else, I face daily the pressure of my con-
cern for all the churches. Who is weak, and I do not
feel weak? Who is led into sin, and I do not inwardly
burn?

Paul knew a thing or two about starving Jesus. Before the Lord knocked him down, he was running hard the other way. He would go on and give the world the value of raw, open, honest testimony about Christ. Paul understood the world needed Jesus. He wasn't going to shut up about Christ. He challenged everyone and was beaten and jailed for it.

11.5 THANK YOU!

You? Where are you? I'm willing to bet a million bucks you have some extra time this week. I'm willing to bet you have an extra five bucks for the basket. I'm thinking you could spend another minute or two on your knees or go without a meal or two this month. What do you think?

Jesus is asking you right now: "Come, follow me." And you say what?

Get up, right now. Stop starving Jesus.

Thanks,

Craig and J.R.

you

the world
(over 2 billion kids)
→

What can you possibly do?

Help ONE.

Get a kid out of poverty for $32 a month.

(800) 336-7676
starvingjesus.com/compassion

Compassion
Releasing children from poverty
in Jesus' name